PRAISE FOR CHALLENGES WON'T STOP ME

"*Challenges Won't Stop Me* is an interactive guide to successfully navigate life. This book provides more than excellent content. It is beautifully illustrated and asks thought-provoking questions for you to journal about. I love how Melony Brown compares camping preparation to preparing for life's obstacles. If you feel like your life is stuck in a rut and you want to become inspired, this book is for you!"

Susan U. Neal RN, MBA, MHS
Author of *7 Steps to Get Off Sugar and Carbohydrates*
Director of the Christian Independent Publishers Association

"*Challenges Won't Stop Me* is by far one of the very best pull yourself up by your bootstraps book I have read in my seventy-five years of living this side of the cross! Having started seminary at the age of forty-seven, I have read hundreds of books on living and dealing with the traumas of life. Never have I thoroughly enjoyed a book about challenges and the struggles to overcome and thrive from a Christian point of view like *Challenges Won't Stop Me*. This book is a gift with great insight. I encourage readers to read and absorb the delicious words of hope Melony Brown shares that are pulled from life and the Holy Scriptures in the Bible. Generously give this book to everyone who crosses your path."

Rev. Deborah Hutchins Koenig McLean
MSB and Licensed Local Pastor

"If life has you stressed and struggling, *Challenges Won't Stop Me* is a must-read. Through practical steps and a fresh perspective, your challenges become manageable and the journey enjoyable. As a life coach, I would highly recommend Melony Brown's book to my clients who are ready to move from survival mode into thriving mode!"

Lori Boruff

Life Coach, Author, Speaker, Christian Communicator Conference Co-director

"You won't just read *Challenges Won't Stop Me* ... you will experience it! Melony Brown not only provides a firm foundation of skills you can immediately use, but you also discover who you are in Christ. Pack up for the journey as Melony guides you through the worst storms of life with wit, wisdom, and HOPE from Almighty God."

Diane Carden

Author, Speaker, Founder of Smart Chick Life

CHALLENGES
WON'T STOP ME

An Interactive Survival Guide
for Overcoming & Thriving

*Journey On!
SERIES
BOOK 1*

*John 16:33
Journey on!
Melony Brown*

MELONY BROWN

FICTION HOUSE PRESS

Challenges Won't Stop Me

Copyright © 2022 by Melony Brown

This title is also available as an eBook and audiobook.

All Scripture quotations, unless otherwise indicated, are taken from The Holy Bible, *New International Version*®, *NIV*®. Copyright © 1973, 1978, 1984, 2011 by Biblica, Inc.® Used by permission. All rights reserved worldwide.

Scripture quotations marked Amplified Bible, Classic Edition are taken from the *Amplified Bible, Classic Edition*. Copyright © 1954, 1958, 1962, 1964, 1965, 1987 by The Lockman Foundation®. Used by permission. All rights reserved.

Scripture quotations marked The Message are taken from *The Message*. Copyright © 1993, 1994, 1995, 1996, 2000, 2001, 2002. Used by permission of NavPress Publishing Group.

Any Internet addresses (websites) in this book are offered as a resource. They are not intended in any way or to imply an endorsement by Fiction House Press, nor does Fiction House Press vouch for the existence, content, or services of these sites, phone numbers, companies, or products beyond the life of this book.

All rights reserved. No part of this publication may be reproduced, stored in a retrieval system, or transmitted in any form or by any means—except for brief quotations in printed reviews, without the prior permission of the publisher.

Brown, Melony, author

Challenges Won't Stop Me: An Interactive Survival Guide for Overcoming & Thriving

Includes biographical references.

ISBN 979-8-9866245-0-1   ISBN 979-8-9866245-1-8 (eBook)

Cover design and interior formatting by *Hannah Linder Designs*

Printed in the United States of America

*For my music man—
Your love and support make my heart sing.
I'm grateful your schedule was free all those years ago.*

CONTENTS

mile 00: Trail Etiquette & Instructions	1
mile 01: How Are You Navigating the Unexpected Turns in Your Journey?	11
mile 02: Is Struggle Really Necessary?	29
mile 03: Where Are You Setting Up Camp?	47
mile 04: Who Is Guiding Your Journey?	63
mile 05: Who Do You Call on When You're Struggling?	79
mile 06: Is Darkness Impeding Your Path?	93
mile 07: Who or What Is Magnified When You See Your Struggles?	107
mile 08: How Will You Remember Your Journey?	123
Rest & Recharge	139
Acknowledgements	147
Appendix of Overcomer Stories	149
Notes	151
Journey On Quiz	155
Keep Moving Forward	157

Trail Etiquette & Instructions

When you set out on a journey and night covers the road, that's when you discover the stars.1
—Nancy Willard, author

A wise woman, seasoned by interesting life experiences, once shared a string of words that nestled deep in my head and heart. She said, "How you live the years allotted to you matters. Your journey matters." Back then, I was too young to understand or appreciate the value of her words. It wasn't until my smooth path gave way to rocky terrain and obstacles impeded my path that I began to fully comprehend her wisdom. Sure, the years I walked a smooth path mattered, but life during those less-challenging years didn't require much navigating. What really mattered during my journey was my mindset, and how I navigated the years marked by tough challenges.

LIVE IN DEFEAT OR FIGHT TO OVERCOME

Her wisdom is too valuable to keep all to myself. So, open your head and heart and receive it: "How you live the years allotted to you matters. Your journey matters." How do you make the years of your journey matter when one of life's tough challenges intersects your path? After you ride the roller coaster of emotions your struggle causes, it's time to evaluate your situation and decide: Will your mindset be to live in defeat or fight to overcome? In distinctly unique ways, both mindsets are powerful indicators of how your struggle will impact the years allotted to you. Choose wisely.

A life lived in lush, grassy meadows with few uphill, rocky paths to challenge you are, well ... safe. But safe doesn't build grit, nor courage, nor fortitude, nor wisdom. A cost is attached to developing these invaluable traits. Some balk at this cost. Others run from it. You are not *some*. And you are not *others*. You are different. Based on the fact you've chosen a book titled *Challenges Won't Stop Me*, I can safely assume you aren't willing to surrender, nor live, in defeat. Neither was I.

At some point, you decided the challenges in your path won't stop you. You've chosen to fight to overcome. Excellent choice! Now, you must consider this question: How do you best navigate your tough challenge? The subtitle of this book— "An Interactive Survival Guide for Overcoming & Thriving "—answers that question. I'm certain you know the meanings of survival, overcome, and thrive. But I want to define them to stress who you and I are fighting to become. *Merriam Webster* defines *survival* as "the act or fact of living or continuing longer than another person or thing; the continuation of life or existence; one who survives." *Overcome* means "to get the better of; surmount." *Thrive* means "to grow vigorously; flourish; to progress toward or realize a goal despite or because of the circumstances." None of those meanings are passive. Instead, active participation is required.

YOUR PERSONALIZED SURVIVAL GUIDE

As you journey through this book, I invite you to actively participate in creating a personalized survival guide. Write notes, observations, and plans for overcoming your tough challenge. Whether you're in the throes of a difficult challenge now or when you face one in the future, your personalized survival guide will be tailor-made to encourage *you* to fight to overcome.

Survival guides are a booming multi-million-dollar industry. Every topic imaginable has been covered, including how to survive buying a home, dealing with toxic people, not killing your houseplants, and even how not to become a crotchety old man! Earning millions is not my goal. Helping you create a survival guide filled with the best tools to overcome your challenges and thrive is!

Don't just read this book. Interact with the content in each mile. Grab different colored pens or highlighters to mark passages. Use colored pencils to color the images throughout the book. No colored pencils? Borrow a handful of your child's crayons! Practice by coloring the tree and birdhouse. Working through each mile quickly isn't the goal. Linger a while, so you can think about and process the sections or Bible verses that speak to you. Don't skip over the questions. Time spent reflecting and then answering the questions will be incredibly valuable to you, revealing truths that will strengthen you for the rest of your journey.

No matter how much you gain from the content I share, the ultimate survival guide is the Bible. As we travel each mile, I will share verses that connect with the topic presented. Even if you've read a verse a dozen times, please read it again. Look for keywords that apply to your current struggle. God *will* speak to you through His words. Slowing down to listen for God's voice is hard, but the payoff is big.

You'll read many Bible verses as we journey together, including a verse that has become my fight verse. I boldly speak it out loud any time a fear or enemy attacks. My fight verse is one of my offensive weapons. You need offensive weapons too. So, be on the lookout for your fight verse. Several verses might be contenders. Put a star by each one or highlight them in a specific color for easy reference. When we reach mile 08, I'll direct you to where to record your fight verse. You'll know you've found your fight verse when it makes your nose scrunch, your teeth clamp together, and your eyes squint when you read it. You might even hear a low growl rumbling in the back of your throat. These reactions occur, because those words resonate with you, filling you with courage, boldness, and determination to fight to overcome whatever struggle *dares* to cross your path.

Additionally, I will share my story and excerpts from the stories of some of the overcomers I've interviewed. Those excerpts summarize the struggle(s) she faced, as well as the lessons she learned. Our stories are diverse, but the commonality of choosing to fight to overcome the challenges impeding our path will encourage you that you are not alone. As you read each excerpt, underline, star, or highlight the parts of that overcomer's story that speaks to you.

A tiny capital letter to the right of each overcomer's name corresponds to the letters on the 'Appendix of Overcomer Stories' page at the back of this book. Beside each letter, you will find the overcomer's first name, the title of her story, the date her story was published, and the word *Story* or *Podcast*. Once you locate the overcomer you'd like to know more about, go to melonybrown.com. Then, click on the *Stories tab* and type the name of her story in the search bar, or click on the *Podcast tab* and scroll to the correct season and episode number.

PACKING YOUR GEAR

It's time to start packing for our journey. Think about the method you use when packing for a trip. Do you pack everything including the kitchen sink or just the essentials? Fold everything neatly or cram everything into your suitcase?

You will need a container to hold all the supplies for your journey. I suggest a backpack. You don't need a literal one. A backpack like this one will do. Each time you come across this visual image, let it remind you that you are gathering valuable and essential gear that will empower you to fight to overcome.

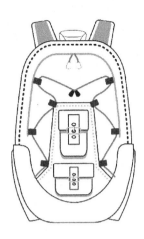

Just as each table, chair, and bookshelf in a tiny house serve a variety of functions, so will each piece of gear we add to our backpacks. This multi-functional gear packs a punch as each piece is meant to be utilized in every area of your life. At each mile marker, I'll introduce a piece of gear and a black and white image representing it. Black and white images of butterflies, birds, the sun, mountains, flowers, etc. will also be scattered throughout this book. Actively participate in creating your survival guide by coloring each of the images. Besides, coloring is fun!

During my decades long health journey, I learned these pieces of gear are not only essential, but they are also helpful. The kind of helpful that kept my mindset strong. The kind of helpful that filled me with unexplainable peace. The kind of helpful that strengthened my resolve to not quit. And the kind of helpful that taught me strategies I would need to fight to overcome.

Am I laying it on too thick? I don't think so. When struggles blocked my path and threatened to defeat me, those pieces of gear were helpful and as trustworthy as a rooster crowing at the sight of the sun beginning to rise. I believe they will be as helpful to you.

THE KIND OF HELPFUL

Maybe like me, you've had a friend who gushed about something that helped her and then she offered it to you. You might have cringed and responded with a kind 'no thanks.' I know I have. Once when this

happened to me, I hastily decided I was doing well in that area, so I dismissed her 'helpful something' as unneeded. Just recently, I assessed the time required to use another friend's 'helpful something' and determined I couldn't add another something to my over-booked schedule. I remember that time I convinced myself the 'helpful something' wouldn't be as helpful to me as it was to my friend because my needs were different than hers. And then there was the time I tried the 'helpful something' for a week or two, and in frustration, tossed it aside when I didn't see immediate results. Just me? Not likely.

In the paragraph above, highlight the four reasons I believed the 'something helpful' offered wasn't for me.

Think of a time when a friend gushed about and then offered you something that helped her. Describe that something she offered. If you tried it, did you find it helpful?

As you learn about the essential pieces of gear, I pray you consider these truths:

- You need these essential pieces of gear even if you are doing well in those areas. Allow the teaching in each of those miles to be a reminder to be persistent in your positive habits.

- Making time for these essential pieces of gear will not add stress to your already crammed schedule. Instead, they will multiply your peace and joy.
- Our needs are as diverse as the colors in a box of 120 Crayola crayons, but these pieces of gear have proven to be helpful to every person with a beating heart.
- You will begin to see noticeable changes when you incorporate the pieces of gear into your daily life, but it's consistency and intentionality that will lead to lasting changes and transformational growth.

When you first looked at the cover of this book, perhaps you felt connected to the outdoorsy image. Journeying together on some trail in the woods is just the kind of break you need. Sleeping under the stars would be a welcome reprieve from the chaos that ensues each night in your home at bedtime. Maybe loneliness invaded your life after your husband passed. You would gladly accept the invitation to connect with nature and a few new friends. Or it could be you're okay with journeying together, but the thought of camping in the woods—in the dirt, with all the bugs, and the lack of proper bathroom facilities—isn't your thing. I understand. Journey during the day and glamp it at night in the nearest luxury hotel or in your blinged out camper instead. Wherever you choose to bunk at night, let's meet by a cozy fire in our pj's to share stories and roast marshmallows. Deal?

TRAIL ETIQUETTE & INSTRUCTIONS

Our journey isn't a thru-hike. We won't cover all the miles of our journey in this book. Instead, a multi-day hike will carry us through the first eight miles. You'll create the second half of your survival guide in book 2. Additional information about book 2 is available at the back of this book. As we embark on this journey, please read the Trail Etiquette & Instruction sign.

Those who have fought to overcome life's tough challenges know the benefits of having support throughout their journey because fighting alone is hard. So, I promise to encourage you when the climb seems too steep or the river too wide to cross. I will support you when a great deal of vulnerability is required to answer the questions I pose. Because your challenges are tough, you must be tougher. You won't hear me sugarcoating how much courage or perseverance you'll need. Know this now: you will need an abundance of both.

When exhaustion hits you hard——and it will—it's not time to quit. Rest instead. Then, dig deep and find an extra boost of energy. Keep moving forward! If you discover you gained a new scar or two during your fight to overcome, remember Ann Voskamp's beautiful words: "Scars are proof you are kind of bullet-proof."[2] I've got quite a few scars, so maybe I'm extra bullet-proof! And when our time together ends, I'll venture as far as to say, you will eagerly agree to journey with a friend or loved one who is struggling and would benefit from your newly learned survival skills.

It's time to hit the trail. Are you feeling expectant or anxious about what's ahead? Travel documentarian, Anthony Bourdain, understood the rub of feeling both expectant and anxious about travel. Instead of focusing on the challenges of the journey ahead, he thought about what he would take away from it and the good he would leave behind. He said, "Travel isn't always pretty. It isn't always comfortable. Sometimes it hurts, it even breaks your heart. But that's okay. The journey changes you—it should change you. It leaves marks on your memory, on your consciousness, on your heart, and on your body. You take something with you. Hopefully, you leave something good behind."[3]

As you turn the page, my prayer for your journey is found in Isaiah 58:11: "The LORD will guide you always; he will satisfy your needs in a sun-scorched land and will strengthen your frame. You will be like a well-watered garden, like a spring whose waters never fail."

Our adventure awaits. Let's journey on!

How Are You Navigating the Unexpected Turns in Your Journey?

> It is this broken road with pitfalls and sharp turns and unexpected traverses that has brought me joy and adventure.1
> — Alice Walker, author of *The Color Purple*

Before we add any gear to our backpacks, we must spend our first mile together addressing the 'elephant in the room.' Because how you live the years allotted to you matters and your journey matters, passively coasting through life doesn't work for you. You knew a detailed plan was necessary to realize your dreams, so you set your course and began making progress. Things were moving along as expected, and then your well-planned path took an unexpected and unwelcome turn.

You weren't expecting it. You don't have time for it. It's unfamiliar territory, yet here you are. It could be you accidentally turned here with that one bad career decision. Or just maybe a chronic health struggle forced a sudden turn. Perhaps, a relationship took a wrong turn that dead ended. It could be that your child was lured onto a path that eventually led to addiction. Our journeys are replete with unexpected turns.

As you read the following paragraph, highlight one or more of the reactions you've experienced because of an unexpected turn in your path.

Encountering an unexpected turn on your well-planned path often invites an assortment of reactions: anger, frustration, confusion, disappointment, uncertainty, shame, anxiety, and loneliness, just to name a few. You might also feel disoriented as you assess this unfamiliar place. Questions arise: Where am I? Who are these people who call themselves friends? How did I get myself into this mess? You likely feel helpless. You wonder how you will get back on your carefully planned path. One of the most common reactions when encountering an unexpected turn is feeling unprepared. That's precisely why we are starting here.

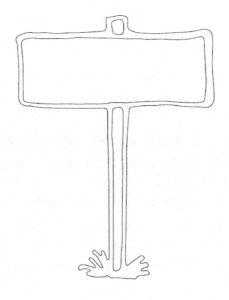

With all these emotions swirling in your head, you might have shouted, "Can't my life just go back to normal?" Unfortunately, no. It's time to assess your current situation and make a new plan that navigates around or through your tough challenge. Trail signs inform and direct, so let's connect this unexpected turn in your journey to the visual image of a trail sign.

CHALLENGES WON'T STOP ME | 13

On the crossroads trail sign below, write one or more events that led to the current unexpected turn in your path.

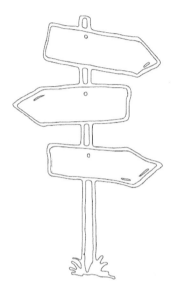

Beside each event you listed above, briefly describe the challenge(s) that followed.

FIGHT TO OVERCOME

Like it or not, we will face unexpected turns at some point in our journey through life. How we respond to those unexpected turns is vitally important. Some shut down. Many will try to survive for a while but eventually give up. Others accept the unexpected turn and decide it won't deter them. They fight to overcome. To understand the backbone needed to fight to overcome, let's look at John 16:33. Jesus said, "In this world you will have trouble. But take heart! I have overcome the world."

Highlight the incredible hope found in this verse.

When we choose to follow Jesus, our troubles in this world T-bone right into Jesus' power living in us. Will our troubles disappear? Maybe. But not likely. Instead, as we step out in faith, He might part the sea like He did for Moses and the Israelites (Exodus 14:21). Perhaps He will be in the fire like He was with Shadrach, Meshach, and Abednego (Daniel 3:13-27). Or it could be that we gain insight and wisdom from our struggle like Paul did with the thorn in his flesh (2 Corinthians 12:7). However God does it, we can choose to hope in Jesus, the One who overcame this world, and trust He's working in and through our troubles.

Jesus overcoming this world is the foundation of my hope. Is He the foundation of your hope?

HOPE LIVING INSIDE YOU

Hope is the confident expectation that God is always with you—an assured reliance that no matter how awful your situation looks, God *will* work it out for your good. We hold tightly to that hope and rely on it. Even though your journey will test you beyond what you think you can endure and challenge you in innumerable ways, I encourage you to believe Jesus *is* with you every step of the way.

When we are fighting to overcome our struggles, why is hope so important? Hebrews 6:19-20 says, "[Now] we have this [hope] as a sure and steadfast anchor of the soul [it cannot *slip* and it cannot *break down* under whoever steps out on it—a hope] that reaches farther and enters into [the very certainty of the Presence] within the veil, where Jesus has entered in for us [in advance]" (AMPC). Because hope is a vital part of our fight to overcome, let's stop for a quick coffee break on the side of the trail and explore these verses a bit.

Please highlight *sure and steadfast* in the verses above.

Merriam Webster defines *sure* as "marked by or given to feelings of confident security; indisputable; firmly established; reliable; trustworthy." And *steadfast* as "firmly fixed in place; not subject to change; firm in belief, determination, or adherence." These definitions characterize our hope in God and His ability to care for us, fight for us, and love us when we face the unexpected turns in our lives.

Underline the parts of the definitions of *sure* and *steadfast* that strengthen your hope and trust in God.

Revisit the verses in Hebrews 6 and highlight *it cannot slip and it cannot break down under whoever steps out on it.*

Slip means "to slide away from one's grasp; to become lost; to decline; to be disengaged from." Our verse though doesn't say our hope slips. It says it *cannot* slip.

After each statement below, write each of the four definitions of *slip*.

1. Hope cannot
2. Hope cannot
3. Hope cannot
4. Hope cannot

Describe how these four statements impact you.

Let's look at one last definition. *Break down* means "to cause to fall or collapse; to make ineffective; to stop functioning; to fail in strength or vitality."

Let's write the cannot version for each definition of *break down*.

1. Hope cannot
2. Hope cannot
3. Hope cannot
4. Hope cannot

Describe how stepping out on this kind of hope could/does impact your struggle.

NEVER LEAVE YOU

If Jesus is your Savior and you follow Him, you have this hope living inside of you. You know the incredible gift hope is. If, on the other hand, you don't know Jesus or haven't chosen to follow Him, may I encourage you to be open to getting to know Him as we journey together? Along each mile, I will share how He isn't up in Heaven looking down on your struggles and merely wishing you well. Quite the opposite. He's walking with you, eager to guide, strengthen, and equip you during your struggles. When you read the Bible verses I share, you will see His character, learn about His promises, and discover He will never leave you. He truly is someone you can count on.

Maybe you don't know what it would look like to have God walk with you during your struggles. Many of the overcomer stories I share will give you a glimpse into what it looks like when He is living and working in you, helping you to navigate your journey. And what it looks like when He is fighting for you. Let's start with my story.

MY HEALTH STRUGGLES [A]

I believe reading my journey of overcoming will ensure you that what I share with you is from a personal understanding of struggle and what it takes to fight to overcome. While I wouldn't have volunteered for my struggles, I'm grateful for everything they've taught me and for my God who has never forsaken me during them.

Memories of the stroke that paralyzed the left side of my body when I was two years old are nonexistent. However, several reminders have walked closely by my side my entire life: residual weakness on my left side, a lack of balance, difficulty with word retrieval, and loving to read but rarely comprehending. Determined my stroke would not define me, my parents expected me to try things kids without challenges did, which included participating in sports. My parents instilled in me an overcomer mindset, which empowered me to navigate around the residual deficits of my stroke. Activities requiring balance and coordination challenged me the most. My left-sided lean fought the bicycle's two wheels until finally I balanced into a wobbly ride around the age of ten.

Throughout my childhood, I struggled with activities which were easy for my peers. The tortoise (me) holding the handrail and taking one deliberate step at a time watched with envy as the hares hopped two or three steps at a time on their way to math class. A passing test grade over the details of a Shakespeare novel required numerous re-readings of the book and studying my notes for days. Anxious thoughts assaulted me every time I thought about taking the required typing class. You see, the fingers on my left-hand work as one unit rather than five individual ones. My parents intervened—the one and only time—and asked if I could exempt the typing class, so my GPA wouldn't take a devastating hit. College presented new academic challenges. But it was during those years I discovered effective strategies that unlocked the way my brain worked, revealing a path that trained me to educate students who struggle academically.

An unexpected turn intersected my path during my first pregnancy: debilitating migraines. A difficult path lay before me. Migraines plagued my late twenties through my late thirties, robbing multiple days of my life with my husband and two young sons. Guilt heaped upon guilt for missing activities with them was the oppressive blanket covering me.

Just a few months before my fortieth birthday, a pile of books slid out of my arms, along with feeling disoriented and having difficulty processing words that were spoken to me. The emergency room doctors assessed me and added a new neurological struggle to my chart: transient ischemic attacks (TIA) or mini strokes. Like lightning hitting a tree time and time again, making the tree weaker and weaker, so was my left side after each subsequent mini stroke. The combined damage to my brain invited an unrelenting fatigue, a bully to be sure. He set up permanent residence.

MOYAMOYA DISEASE

After the fourth TIA, my neurologist referred me to a neurosurgeon who ordered an angiogram of my brain. The images showed a tangle of blood vessels on my right middle cerebral artery (MCA), which validated and explained: (1) the stroke at age two, (2) the decade+ years of debilitating migraines, and (3) the series of TIAs. My neurological conditions met the three (and only three) criteria for Moyamoya* disease.

*Moyamoya disease is a rare, progressive cerebrovascular disease caused by blocked arteries in the brain. The name "Moyamoya" means puff of smoke in Japanese and describes the tangle of tiny vessels formed in the brain to compensate for the blockage. It affects 1 in 2,000,000 people.

As crazy as it may sound, it was a relief to finally have explanations and a name for the neurological struggles I'd faced throughout my life. Research confirmed my neurosurgeon's recommendation that brain surgery was the best treatment option to stop or slow my progressive disease. Adding new neurological struggles throughout my life were certainly unexpected turns in my path but processing the fact that I would be having brain surgery took me to my knees. I knew it was time to navigate this unfamiliar territory. I was determined to fight to overcome.

TAKE MY OWN MEDICINE

Every possible way the surgery could go wrong looped endlessly in my brain, yet I knew I couldn't remain there. Repeating my life verse over and over put my focus on God instead of on my upcoming surgery. It says, "My trust and assured reliance and confident hope *shall be fixed in Him*" (Hebrews 2:13 AMPC, emphasis mine). Because my mindset of fighting to overcome was intricately linked to remaining fixed on Him, this verse also became my fight verse. I could be a bully too. I decided to be just as aggressive and unrelenting as my fatigue in repeating aloud and believing the words in my fight verse.

A few weeks before my surgery, I came across a quote by inspirational writer, Caroline Naorgi, which says, "Your testimony is richer when the test is harder."[2] Brain surgery did seem like an exceptionally hard test. What if how I prepared for and took this test became my testimony? I teach my students a crucial part of preparing well for a test is repeating information out loud to get it sticky in your brain. "Repetition is your friend" is the motto I teach. It was time to take my own medicine.

The four-and-a-half-hour indirect brain bypass surgery allowed my neurosurgeon to move a thriving blood vessel from above my right ear and graft it into the area of my brain that was not receiving adequate blood flow. A truly modern miracle if you ask me! In the recovery room, I decided the hardest part of the test was behind me because I could follow conversations, respond, and eat. I passed the test! There is no doubt in my mind that God was with me during every unexpected turn on my neurological journey, including the turn that led to brain surgery.

I am incredibly grateful for my husband Jeff's unconditional love and support throughout my decades of struggle. When he describes my brain surgery to someone unfamiliar with my story, he says, "Yeah, she updated her hardware, and now she has a supercharged brain!" While his proclamation is funny, I truly believe God did update my hardware, supercharging my brain, so I can support and encourage others to fight to overcome the challenges that intersect their paths.

When I look back over the years since my brain surgery, I cannot help but marvel at everything God has done and is doing in my body, my brain, and my life. I'm not a Pollyanna, spouting off how wonderfully easy life is now. The truth is my path hasn't been perfectly smooth since then. I've encountered a few bumps along the way. To keep my mindset strong, I wrote this "fight song" to embolden me to keep fighting: Moyamoya disease will not defeat me, nor will it stop me from pursuing all God has in store for me.

Perhaps my fight song can be your fight song too. Personalize it by filling in the blank with your struggle.

_____ will not defeat me, nor will it stop me from pursuing all God has in store for me.

Put a sticky note on the edge of this page and label it fight song, so you can easily find it when you need it. Sing it, and even shout it, when you feel like giving up.

WHERE SHE WILL BECOME STRONG

Now that you know a little about my unexpected turns, let's consider why those unwelcome turns intersect our path. Luke Easter's poem, "A Strong Woman Vs. A Woman of Strength," describes how struggles in a woman's journey build strength: "A strong woman has faith that for the journey she'll have enough, no matter how uneven the terrain or roads being rocky and rough, a woman of strength knows it's in the journey she will become strong, and the love of God is forever with her, no matter how difficult or long."[3]

Double underline *it's in the journey she will become strong*. **Describe how this applies to you and your journey.**

You and I will develop strength *in* the unexpected turns in our journey. I don't develop strength when the biggest health struggle I face is a stuffy nose during spring allergy season. Nor will I develop strength when every project I launch is hugely successful. And I certainly won't develop strength when work bonuses show up in Jeff's paycheck month after month.

I develop strength when I fight to recover after new neurological health challenges. When I launch a new ministry project and it fails, my strength grows. Lastly, I develop strength when skinny paychecks remind me that needs and wants are vastly different things. Developing strength is hard. But remember this: each time we commit to developing strength during the hard times, we are becoming women of strength. My real-life examples of how I have developed strength through struggles with my health, with a ministry project, and with our finances were shared to get you thinking.

Describe three unexpected struggles you've faced, recording them in chronological order from oldest to most recent. After each struggle, record a strength you developed as a result.

1.

2.

3.

Now highlight each strength you recorded above. Write each strength in the flow chart below.

Do you see a connection between the strength you needed in the second struggle and what you gained in the first? Describe it.

Is there a connection between the strength you needed in the third struggle and what you gained in the first and second struggles? Describe it.

ONE PHONE CALL

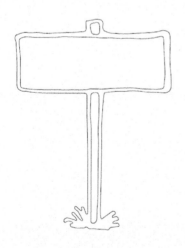

Julie's [B] story is a beautiful example of how the challenges that come with an unexpected turn can also include joy and adventure. Three years into their marriage, Julie and Stephen decided they were ready to expand their family. Excitement about having a baby consumed their daily conversations. Their hopes were dashed when her menstrual cycle appeared month after month. The word infertile, for a woman who desperately wanted to be a mother, was a devastating unexpected turn. Several natural treatments were tried, but none were effective. Like a stretched rubber band, their faith was tested and tried. "Why not us?" was the unanswered question that punctured holes in their hope.

Julie questioned her worth as a woman when four inseminations failed to lead to a pregnancy. Rock bottom hit hard. A suggestion to consider adoption infused Julie and Stephen with new hope. Just as each monthly cycle had crushed Julie, so did each month of a birth mother not choosing them to adopt her child. A year of grief for their unrealized dream caused Julie and Stephen to question if this new road also led to a dead end.

One phone call would change their lives forever. A baby boy needed a forever home. "Are you and Stephen interested?" asked the adoption case worker. With a resounding "Yes," their pit of despair became a chorus of very loud praise. "The moment I held him in my arms as my own son, I was madly in love with him," Julie shared. "All the struggles we'd been through were worth every minute." They experienced joy intermingled with the challenges. Only God could be responsible for sending a son who so closely resembles his adopted dad.

You see, the one who wanted to be a mother didn't have to give birth to have children. That unexpected turn took her exactly where God wanted her to be. Joy and adventure were found as she and Stephen immersed themselves in their son's academic journey, in his extracurricular activities, and most importantly in his spiritual development. Her son is thriving in college and is pursuing his dreams. Julie's dream of children isn't limited to her son. She isn't just a mom to her son. Julie "mothers" and mentors dozens of young girls in the youth group at her church. Countless young people have benefitted immensely from Julie's motherly love for them.

SET MY MIND

I'm certain I have not convinced you to love the sight of an unexpected turn in your journey. I don't love them either. Knowing unexpected turns are part of your life journey and keeping your mindset strong enables you to be as prepared for them as possible. As I worked on the revisions for this chapter, another unexpected turn disrupted my path: my colon flipped upside down and became obstructed, which led to an emergency surgery. Chalk up another rare disease for me!

The words in this mile were fresh in my mind. I wasn't expecting this unexpected turn. I didn't have time for it. And because an issue with my colon wasn't my usual neurological struggles, I was in unfamiliar territory. Yet here I was. Once again, it was time to take my own medicine.

I pulled out my life verse and proclaimed: "My trust, assured reliance, and confident hope are fixed in Him." I set my mind on these truths, so I was ready when the enemy launched an attack on me during my five-day hospital stay. Oh, how strategic he is. The fiery arrows he shot at me were meant to entice me to give up and not fight to overcome. But the enemy doesn't know me as well as he thought he did! I'm a fighter. I'm an overcomer. Studying God's Word daily strengthened and equipped me for this unexpected turn and attack of the enemy. With God and His Word on my side, we counterattacked with power and light! The enemy bowed in defeat and scurried back to his dark pit.

If you have a life verse, write it below.

If you don't have a life verse, I highly recommend picking one. Because I've repeated my life verse so many times over the years, it pops in my mind at just the right moment, exactly when I need to be reminded of those powerful truths. Your life verse may be one which speaks loudly of hope. It could be one which helps you navigate your journey because how you live the years of your life matters. Perhaps it's one that fortifies you during tough times. May the words of your life verse—God's truth—work powerfully in you when your path is smooth *and* when it's rocky.

The trail sign marks this unexpected turn in your journey. Getting stuck here is not an option. Now, it's time to navigate the path ahead. Grab your backpack. At the next mile marker, we will begin adding the essential gear you'll need for your journey of overcoming.

Each of us may be sure that if God sends us over rocky paths, He will provide us with sturdy shoes. He will never send us on any journey without equipping us well.4

—Alexander Maclaren, Scottish Baptist minister

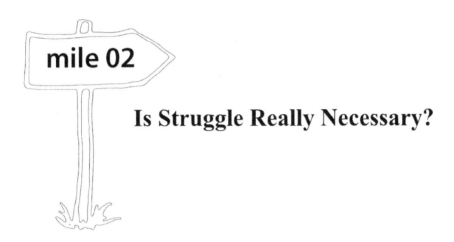

Is Struggle Really Necessary?

The struggle of life is one of our greatest blessings. It makes us patient, sensitive, and Godlike. It teaches us that although the world is full of suffering, it is also full of overcoming it.1

—Helen Keller, author and disability rights advocate

Struggle is necessary. Really? Better to rip off the bandage now, so the hurt, frustration, anger, and dare I say offense, you feel about your struggle will not grow or get infected. What thoughts come to mind when you hear the word struggle? Maybe you envision strain, sweat, pain, difficulty, stumbling, long suffering, opposition, and even warfare. You may not be ready to admit all those words in the last sentence are necessary for our growth, but they are.

NOT STRONG ENOUGH

My guess is you are currently facing a tough struggle. Likely, you've talked about it with your spouse, best friend, or dog. We have, too. Take a look.

Dear STRUGGLE,

    I don't want to give you the time of day, much less a cheery greeting. I'll save us time by getting right to the point. Who invited you? Certainly not me. Why did you choose ME? I am weak. I'm not strong enough to survive this. You've cast a dark cloud over my life. I can't break free. I'm full of rage at the trouble you're causing.

    Sleepless nights accumulate quickly as I weep over what has happened to me. Thoughts of what I should do about you roll around in my head all night. There are no answers. The weariness you cause is unbearable. You are physically, mentally, and emotionally painful and exhausting. I saw rock bottom coming, but I was powerless to stop it. Everything is piling up on me all at once. The weight is oppressive.

    No one understands me. I feel the stabbing words of condemnation when people point out what a wreck I am. My friends and family are weary of hearing my woes. Some have deserted me. Their rejection stings. You've forced me to keep my feelings to myself. I'm alone in my suffering. You take and you take some more. You take health from my bones. You take vitality and vigor from my personality. You take years from my life as I have no choice but to focus on you. When will enough be enough? I'm done with this ridiculous idea of long-suffering. I need a break!

    Feeling trapped amongst the tentacles of financial loss, the strain on my marriage, my weakened body, and a cluttered mind is truly hell on earth. I can't fix this myself. I am drowning in despair. You've changed me so much I don't even recognize myself. When I think about how much energy it takes to fight you, I decide defeat won't be so bad. I can't live like this anymore. You've won. Isn't that your goal?

                                    Ungratefully yours,
                                       ME

Would it surprise you to learn those raw and vulnerable words are a conglomeration of comments from the 135+ overcomers I've interviewed regarding the struggles they faced? We've been there. Again, I say you are not alone.

I invite you to interact with the letter above. Highlight or underline or draw unhappy faces next to the statements you identify with in the Dear struggle letter. If those statements miss the mark in describing your struggles, write your own here.

Dear struggle,

Ungratefully,

THE GREATEST STRESS YOU CAN BEAR

This may feel like a stretch, but let's connect the idea of struggle to a rope. Perhaps defining the word rope will help you see the connection. A *rope* is a group of yarns, fibers, or strands braided or twisted together for the purposes of dragging, causing resistance/opposition, or lifting.

Braiding or twisting yarns, fibers, or strands are what gives rope its strength. Specifically, tensile strength, which is the greatest longitudinal stress a substance can bear without tearing apart. Suppose our struggles mimic the tensile strength of a rope. Your struggle is the greatest stress you can bear without tearing apart. When a rope is used, its strength is tested. The stronger the rope, the less likely the rope will tear apart, no matter the amount of stress put upon it.

ARMS ME WITH STRENGTH

I imagine connecting struggle to the first two purposes of a rope—dragging and causing resistance/opposition — isn't a big leap. Most of us have experienced one or both. We know dragging isn't something you choose for yourself; instead, it's acted upon you by an outside force. Being drug through an unwanted divorce or through years of infertility or through the lies someone is spreading about you is painful. The stress threatens to tear you apart.

Opposition and resistance are synonyms. Both mean a hostile or contrary action. These can be either an outside force or an inside force, causing or contributing to your struggle. Resistance and opposition because of an ex-spouse's unwillingness to share custody of your child or ongoing, unresolved conflict in a relationship with a family member are tremendously taxing struggles. Encountering roadblocks or an unwillingness to compromise when starting or expanding a business or project may feel like a tearing apart of your dreams.

Close your eyes for a moment and picture your struggle. Is your struggle dragging you, resisting you, or opposing you? Describe how it is tearing you apart.

CHALLENGES WON'T STOP ME | 33

Write *struggle/strength* **just above this coil of rope. To the left of it, write** *the greatest stress you can bear without tearing apart.* **To the right of it, write** *purposes are to drag, cause resistance/opposition, and lift.*

NO MATTER THE AMOUNT OF STRESS

Whether your struggles are dragging you or you are experiencing opposition and resistance, the stress, exhaustion, and frustration consuming you often lead to feeling as if you are being tested beyond what you can endure. This is the point at which your tensile strength—the greatest longitudinal stress a substance can bear without tearing apart—is being tested. You might resist and/or fight hard, but you can't overcome this struggle in your own strength. Thankfully, we can ask for and rely on God's strength. Inviting Him to be braided and twisted in us is what gives us strength. Remember: the stronger the rope, the less likely the rope will tear apart—no matter the amount of stress it endures.

Adversaries attacked King David frequently. Even though he had well-trained armies with the strongest soldiers, it would take much more to defeat his enemies. He knew where his strength came from: "It is God who arms me with strength and keeps my way secure" (Psalm 18:32).

Are you relying on God to arm you with strength? If so, describe what that looks like.

LIFT US OUT

The third purpose of a rope is lifting. You likely know *lifting* means "to raise from a lower to a higher position; to ascend; to rise." Think of a calf that fell in a ditch. It was powerless to save itself and needed rescuing. Someone noticed its need, tied a rope around its waist, and lifted it out of the ditch.

You will need rescuing when you fall or get shoved into a ditch. You are powerless to save yourself. God notices your need and desires to lift you out of the ditch. You and I would do well not to wave Him away, saying, "I've got this. I don't need your help." When He tells us our posture is working against us and asks us to turn this way or that, His method of lifting us out will go smoother if we cooperate. God will take on the heavy lifting. Trust Him.

King David sinned. Accepting the mess he'd made, he sought God's strength to lift him out: "He lifted me out of the slimy pit, out of the mud and mire; he set my feet on a rock and gave me a firm place to stand" (Psalm 40:2).

In the moment, you might not have realized it was God lifting you up when you were struggling with sin, or when you struggled with a burden or a health struggle. Now that you can look back and see it, briefly describe that time and how God lifted you up.

UNEXPECTED AND UNIMAGINABLE TURN

As you read Eva's story, highlight the dragging, the resistance/opposition, and the lifting she experienced.

Ms. Eva's ᶜ father met resistance and opposition when in 1939 his business license was revoked in Czechoslovakia. The reason? He was Jewish. Only two years old at the time, her family fled to Budapest, Hungary to start over. Several years later when she was in first grade, she encountered opposition at her school when it was announced that Jewish children weren't allowed to recite the Hungarian pledge.

That same year, her father was dragged away to a forced labor camp. News reached their home that he had been killed. This unexpected and unimaginable turn would test her family's tensile strength. Could they bear this stress without tearing apart? Along with thousands of other Jewish people, Eva, her mother, and her sister were forced to live in the Budapest ghettos. The residents of the ghettos were the old, the sick, the women, and the children of Jewish heritage.

Eva's mother, Gisella, fought to protect Eva and her sister, Violet. Unfortunately, Gisella couldn't resist the Hungarian guards who drug her out in the middle of the night. Eva and Violet were left to fend for themselves. A month later, the girls were led to the Danube River. They watched in horror as others were told to remove their shoes and then fell into the river after being shot. Seven-year-old Eva believed this would be how her life would end.

But it didn't end there. Eva described her rescue—her lifting out—as a miracle. "My mother heard my sister's crying voice, ran to the river, and bribed a German guard with her wedding band to release her children. What we didn't know until later is that after being captured, our mother escaped from the train, hid in the woods for several days, and made her way back to the ghetto to rescue us. She is my hero."

HELPED US HEAL

Several years later, a mutual friend introduced Eva to a handsome Holocaust survivor named Les. Eva and Les were married after two months of courting. When a revolution broke out in Hungary that same year, they knew it was time to navigate a new path. Les, Eva, and Les' parents escaped over the border into Austria and joined other refugees who immigrated to the United States.

Because Eva and Les lost so many family members in the Holocaust, they were overjoyed when their son and daughter were born. For thirty-nine years of their marriage, they didn't talk about their Holocaust experiences as it was just too painful. Finally, in 1989, Eva and Les began sharing their stories with audiences across the nation, proclaiming the truth that the Holocaust happened. "Doing those talks helped us heal," Eva shared. "I will never forget what happened to us. And I never want to forget it because it made me who I am. It's part of my life."

In 2021, Les passed away. In a recent conversation with this beautiful and joyful eighty-five-year-old woman, Eva shared she misses Les terribly and is grateful for all her years with him. She intends to enjoy activities and making memories with her children, grandchildren, and great-grandson for many years to come.

YOUR CURRENT SUFFERINGS

Just as Ms. Eva has known suffering, the apostle Paul knew it too. He was beaten, shipwrecked, stoned, hungry, attacked, robbed, snake-bitten, and thrown in prison multiple times. He also endured a 'thorn in his flesh.'

Paul, having endured all these sufferings, understood the dragging, the resistance, and the oppositions he faced would one day be met with God lifting him up to Heaven. He described why he could endure all of it in Romans 8:18. He confidently wrote, "I consider that our present sufferings are not worth comparing to the glory that will be revealed in us."

Whoa. Reread that verse and highlight it.

Let's remember those words the next time we are dragged or face resistance/opposition. And don't forget He will lift you up to Heaven one day.

In the space below, list your current or past sufferings. You're not sharing this list with anyone, so be open and transparent. After you list your sufferings, think of heaven. Now, describe the glory you hope will be revealed in you, redeeming each of your sufferings.

Current/past Struggle

1.
2.
3.

Glory Revealed

1.
2.
3.

THE SOURCE OF OUR STRUGGLES

You might have a name for your struggle, but that name isn't who or what is causing your pain. We must identify the source of our struggles. In Ephesians 6, Paul points out *who* is causing your struggles.

Read Ephesians 6:12 and underline who your struggles are against.

> "For our struggle is not against flesh and blood, but against the rulers, against the authorities, against the powers of this dark world and against the spiritual forces of evil in the heavenly realms."

The remainder of Ephesians 6 explains the defensive and offensive weapons you must use to defeat the true source of our struggles. Those weapons are not the physical weapons you think of when the military fights terror, or a knight defends the honor of his lady, or a man uses to kill an animal to provide dinner for his family. These weapons are spiritual and are far more powerful.

As you read Ephesians 6:13-18, highlight the defensive and offensive weapons Paul describes.

Therefore put on the full armor of God, so that when the day of evil comes, you may be able to stand your ground, and after you have done everything, to stand. Stand firm with the belt of truth buckled around your waist, with the breastplate of righteousness in place, and with your feet fitted with the readiness that comes from the gospel of peace. In addition to all this, take up the shield of faith, with which you can extinguish all the flaming arrows of the evil one. Take the helmet of salvation and the sword of the Spirit, which is the word of God. And pray in the Spirit on all occasions with all kinds of prayers and requests. With this in mind, be alert and always keep on praying for all the Lord's people.

Below, create an easily accessible reference of the **VERY POWERFUL** weapons God gives you to use when Satan attacks.

DEFENSIVE WEAPONS

1.
2.
3.
4.
5.

OFFENSIVE WEAPONS

6.
7.

These weapons are spiritual weapons, given to us by our loving Father. He knows physical weapons will not defeat Satan and his armies. The only weapons which will truly defeat Satan are the defensive weapons of truth, righteousness, peace, faith, salvation, and the offensive weapons of the Word of God and prayer. When you wield these weapons, the God of the universe and His armies fight for you!

God has given you the only weapons that will defeat the struggles Satan puts in your life. Are you consistently using them? If not, why not?

SUBTLE AT FIRST

Just a year after her youngest child was born, Cheryl D noticed her left eyelid drooped and her left foot would drag while she was walking. "It was subtle at first," she explained. "I didn't have time to think about it. On the days it happened, I decided not to think about the weird feeling in my leg. Later in the day, I'd realize that weird feeling was gone." Cheryl would forget about it until it happened again.

The weird symptoms persisted, so she made an appointment with her primary care doctor to discuss her concerns. Brain fog and fatigue were added to the list. Cheryl found it difficult to describe her symptoms. They were so unfamiliar to the then thirty-three-year-old woman who had been the epitome of good health. Her doctor listened, but replied, "Well, of course, you have brain fog and fatigue. You're caring for four young children." His response rattled her. Cheryl believed her symptoms were more than being an overly tired mother. Worried the consistent left-sided weakness in her arm and leg might be stroke symptoms, she went to the emergency room. The ER doctor described her test results as in 'the normal range' and laughed off her concerns. "It was demoralizing to not have my symptoms taken seriously."

GIVE YOURSELF GRACE

Desperate for a medical professional to determine the cause for her symptoms and help her navigate this unexpected path, Cheryl underwent a barrage of tests at Northwestern University. The neurologist reviewed the test results with her, pointing out that all the results were 'in the normal range.' "There is nothing physically wrong with you," he said. "I would recommend you see a psychiatrist." Once again, Cheryl felt defeated and lost, helpless and hopeless. She knew whatever was happening in her body, making her weak and fatigued, was not something she made up in her head. It was real. But all the doctors said nothing was wrong, so she believed, "I'm just going to have to live this way with no help and no hope."

When she was at her lowest, a friend reminded her that Job, during his hardest days, declared, "But he knows the way that I take; when he has tested me, I will come forth as gold" (Job 23:10). "I began seeing the gold through my struggles. Not in spite of my struggles, but through them." Finally, after eight months of consistent symptoms and even more testing, a neurologist who took her concerns seriously, diagnosed her with myasthenia gravis (MG), a chronic autoimmune disorder. Cheryl began antibody infusion treatments, replenishing the antibodies that were being destroyed by MG. Having this diagnosis meant her symptoms were indeed real, but it took a while to process that this illness isn't one that experiences full healing.

Over the last twenty-three years, Cheryl's experienced several flare-ups, as well as periods of remission. She has learned to listen to her body and rest when needed. While stress cannot be completely avoided, she takes the advice a nurse practitioner offered her: "Your body handles stress differently than someone without a neurological condition, so you have to give yourself grace." She extends this grace to herself, but she realized she must also extend it to others who are struggling.

Cheryl readily admits while she never would have asked for MG, she believes God has allowed it to deepen her compassion and desire to help others. Since 2012, Cheryl desires to serve those who need rest in God's embrace through her writing and speaking ministry, Securely Held. It's based on the truth found in Deuteronomy 33:12: "Let the beloved of the Lord rest secure in him, for he shields him all day long, and the one the Lord loves rests between his shoulders." Cheryl is writing a series of books based on what she's learned from her struggles with a focus on finding significance and security in God's embrace.

Describe what giving yourself grace when you're struggling would look like.

INWARDLY WE ARE BEING RENEWED

Before we finish walking this mile, let's look at Paul's insights about what God's power does in us when we go through earthly struggles. Second Corinthians 4:7-9 says, "But we have this treasure in jars of clay to show that this all-surpassing power is from God and not from us. We are hard pressed on every side, but not crushed; perplexed, but not in despair; persecuted, but not abandoned; struck down, but not destroyed."

In the verses above, underline *hard pressed, perplexed, persecuted,* and *struck down*. Now highlight *but not crushed, but not in despair, but not abandoned,* and *but not destroyed.*

Describe how enduring the underlined words and living out the highlighted words demonstrates God's all-surpassing power in your life.

In these verses, Paul explained how unbelievers' eyes are veiled to the truth. Perhaps one purpose of our struggles is so an unbeliever will see how Christ-followers are hard-pressed, perplexed, persecuted, or struck down, but we aren't crushed, in despair, abandoned, or destroyed.

Just a few verses later, Paul wrote, "Therefore we do not lose heart. Though outwardly we are wasting away, yet inwardly we are being renewed day by day. For our light and momentary troubles are achieving for us an eternal glory that far outweighs them all. So we fix our eyes not on what is seen, but on what is unseen, since what is seen is temporary, but what is unseen is eternal" (vs. 16-18).

Your physical body is wasting away to age, disease, addiction, abuse, neglect. But inwardly (where your spiritual body is), you are being renewed day by day. As your physical body is growing older and more worn out, your spiritual body is growing younger and more refreshed. How incredible is that trade!

LIGHT AND MOMENTARY

In those verses, Paul described our troubles as light and momentary. Those adjectives are hard to swallow. For some of us, we've dealt with our struggles for decades. Decades hardly seem momentary. Instead of focusing on, worrying about, or trying to control your struggles, Paul implores you to fix your eyes on Jesus.

Look at Romans 8:18 again: "I consider that our present sufferings are not worth comparing to the glory that will be revealed in us." Compare it with 2 Corinthians 4:16-18: "Therefore we do not lose heart. Though outwardly we are wasting away, yet inwardly we are being renewed day by day. For our light and momentary troubles are achieving for us an eternal glory that far outweighs them all. So we fix our eyes not on what is seen, but on what is unseen, since what is seen is temporary, but what is unseen is eternal."

What theme do they have in common?

Those verses promise eternal glory, which you will receive when you are lifted to heaven! The dragging, as well as the resistance and opposition your earthly struggles put you through, will achieve eternal glory in Heaven. Even though we could chat for days about everything that entails, let's not linger. We have more gear to pack.

When you come to the end of your rope, tie a knot and hang on.2

—An American West proverb

Where Are You Setting Up Camp?

God's love does not protect us from suffering. God's love protects us in the midst of suffering.1
—Hans Kung, Catholic priest and theologian

Georgia rarely experiences zero-degree weather with negative 19 windchills, even in the dead of winter. But that first year Jeff and I were married, he and his friend, Mike, eagerly challenged the predicted forecast so as not to miss their guy's weekend backpacking trip. Sleeping in a flimsy tent with such frigid temperatures seemed dangerous to me. A week of pleading with him to not go fell into the nagging wife category. Jeff listened but confidently assured me he and Mike would be fine. (Disclaimer: Georgia winters don't even remotely compare to winters in the northern United States. But for us Georgians, those temperatures and conditions are COLD.)

Unwilling to look like wimps, Jeff and Mike arrived fully prepared to tackle the cold and traversed down Tallulah Gorge. Darkness encroached. Howling wind bounced off the sheer walls of the gorge, making it necessary to quickly pitch their tent on the first flat surface they found. Upon waking from a frigid night in a tent deemed appropriate for summer use, Jeff and Mike resembled human icicles.

Jeff crawled out of the tent first. A fifty-foot-tall frozen waterfall greeted him. The morning sun had already begun to melt the edges. Small chunks of the frozen waterfall fell as he and Mike disassembled their tent. Thankfulness for narrowly escaping disaster should have been on their lips. But it wasn't. Instead, they couldn't stop laughing. Laughter and granola bar crumbs trailed behind them as they hiked to their next destination. In comparison, the rest of the weekend was uneventful.

Since this trip occurred pre-cell phones, I fretted away at home, wondering if my man would need multiple days to thaw. When he finally made it home, Jeff shared how they narrowly avoided trouble as huge shards of the waterfall could have fallen on them while they slept. *All because of where they pitched their tent.*

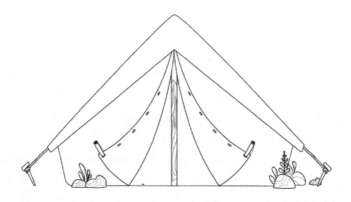

As you might have already guessed, our visual image for this chapter is a tent. We will look at the best place to pitch your tent, as well as discover the purposes of a tent.

THE TROUBLES YOU'RE FACING

Just out of curiosity, I looked up the word *trouble* in my *Flip Dictionary*.[2] I call it my thesaurus on steroids. My students hate it when I pull it out. Here's why: I found seventy-six synonyms for trouble. That number made me pause. No matter if you call your trouble adversity, crisis, dilemma, grief, misfortune, strife, or woe, it will impede your path and *it will have to be addressed*. Ignoring your trouble isn't an option.

The troubles you're facing on your journey are not likely a one-day event. Its duration could be weeks, months, years, or even decades.

Trouble comes in many forms: an unexpected health diagnosis, the loss of a job and the financial security it provided, an abusive relationship, poor friendship choices, fears that incapacitate, an addiction that controls your life, the death of a child or spouse, or a mental illness that invades every area of your life.

Do you identify with any of those troubles? Circle them. If not, write your trouble(s) below.

Having your specific trouble in mind as we proceed will assure you reap the most benefits from this mile of our journey.

WHERE YOU SEEK SHELTER IS A CRUCIAL DECISION

There are only two places to go when we run into trouble: the world's shelter or God's shelter. Where you choose to stake your tent during times of trouble determines what kind of protection, refuge, and rest you will receive.

If you stake your tent in an unhealthy relationship, bruises, fractured bones, and a wounded spirit will leave you cowering and broken. Consistently stake your tent across from a bartender or in the contents of a lighted spoon, and your body will shrivel to a carcass. Stake your tent in a minefield of fear and worst-case scenarios, and destruction will cloud your vision. The world's shelter is flimsy, holey, and damaged.

Subduing the bone-chilling cold can't be found within the walls of the world's tent. This shelter doesn't provide any protection at all. Weary from months of treatment? Too bad. Maybe you're hoping for a little refuge from your enemies. Nope, not here. The paper-thin walls of the world's tent won't drown out the incessant doomsday predictions of naysayers who predict you won't survive or overcome your struggle.

Maybe you've never thought about the poor quality of the world's protection and the fact that it offers minimal refuge. A tent staked in the world leaves you exposed and vulnerable. I'm not a blunt person, but I'll venture there to make this point: Why would you choose the world's shelter?

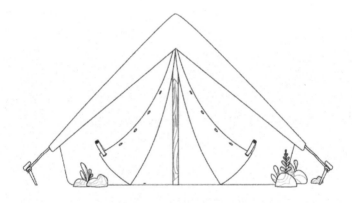

Perhaps you know God's shelter is where you need to be during your struggles, but you've forgotten why. Please allow me to remind you. God's shelter is solid, reliable, and effective. Run to it and find an all-weather covering that shields you from the relentless, pounding rains of your ongoing struggles. Howling winds of failure and not being enough cramming your ears full of lies? God's helmet of salvation will protect your mind and your life from the enemy's schemes. Wrapping a warm blanket of God's love around you will push away the loneliness from broken relationships or suffocating depression, providing the refuge you're so desperate to have. Weary from the fatigue that comes with chronic illness? Unzip God's tent and experience true rest that is healing, refreshing, and energizing.

Regarding your current struggle, which tent have you chosen?

GIVING GOD THE GLORY

In the aftermath of a tornado that ransacked her home in 2010, several news reporters interviewed Tami [E]. Her fifteen-year-old daughter, Jordyn, overheard her giving God the glory for her safety and those who were also in the home with her during the tornado. Later that day, Jordyn asked, "Would you be giving God the glory if me or one of our family members died?" Tami quickly responded, "Well honey, just like in that VeggieTales episode[3] with Rack, Shack, and Bennie, I would be faithful even if He does not."

Jordyn listened to Tami's response, nodded to show she understood, and went on her way. Tami couldn't just go on her way. Her too quick response haunted her, causing her to question everything about her faith. She realized she did not have the faith she claimed to live by. God beckoned Tami to find her *even if He does not* faith. In obedience, she sought refuge in God's tent. Over the next year, Tami experienced a deep friendship with God as she began diligently studying His Word and connecting with Him in prayer more frequently.

Time in God's tent fortified her faith and prepared her for the next ten years, which brought even more challenging situations. In two of those situations, Tami struggled to understand why Jordyn stepped away from her faith and why her dad died unexpectedly in a boat explosion. Each situation resulted in loss and deep grief. But Tami knew to run to God's tent. Each time, God met her with open arms.

EVEN IF HE DOES NOT FAITH

Nine years after the tornado ravaged her home, a doctor diagnosed Jordyn, now twenty-four years old, with stage 4 Sarcoma, which ravaged Tami's heart. What an unexpected turn this was. Questions swirled in her mind about why her daughter, so young and vibrant and adventurous, must suffer. The diagnosis rocked Jordyn's world too, causing her to run back to God's tent. Tami and Jordyn clung to Jordyn's favorite verse, Philippians 4:13, which says, "I can do all things through him who gives me strength." Tami spent time in God's tent, asking Him to help her navigate this new path.

She wasn't surprised when Jordyn chose to receive her chemo treatments while exploring the United States in an RV. During those days on the road, Jordyn stepped back toward God and drew upon His strength, as well as the truths she learned about God as a child. Jordyn shared a concern that Tami's prayers weren't focused on the realities of her diagnosis and prognosis. She reminded Tami she needed to find her *even if he does not* faith. The kind of faith three faithful God-followers professed in Daniel 3 when King Nebuchadnezzar threatened to throw them in a blazing furnace if they did not worship his gods. In response to the king's threat, Shadrach, Meshach, and Abednego replied, "If we are thrown into the blazing furnace, the God we serve is able to deliver us from it, and he will deliver us from Your Majesty's hand. But *even if he does not*, we want you to know, Your Majesty, that we will not serve your gods or worship the image of gold you have set up" (Daniel 3: 17-18, emphasis mine).

Tami decided to fully surrender to God's plan for Jordyn. A few months before Jordyn passed, she returned home to receive hospice. Mother and daughter soaked up every minute in conversation and laughter. When Jordyn transitioned to be with God, Tami felt an unspeakable joy knowing Jordyn was no longer suffering and was with God. "While I will spend the rest of my days grieving the loss of my sweet girl, I now know that my faith is sure even though He did not change the narrative I prayed for." After Jordyn's funeral, Tami ran right into God's tent for the kind of rest only He could give.

It's been a year since Jordyn's passing. Tami has already seen the first harvests from her precious daughter dying. She plans to write a book about her journey of finding her *even if he does not* faith. She enjoys helping clients update their homes with interior design that reflects their personalities.

Don't rush this moment. Think about the struggles you have faced or are facing now. If God does not provide the healing, restoration, forgiveness, or opportunities you've prayed for, do you have *even if he does not* faith?

GOD'S TENT OFFERS REFUGE/PROTECTION

No matter the struggles you face, you can run straight into God's tent, confident He will receive you every single time. His tent serves two trustworthy purposes: refuge/protection and a safe place to rest.

Whether you're at the beginning, middle, or nearing the end of your troubles, you need His refuge/protection and a place to rest.

Is the enemy attacking you on every side? You need God's refuge and protection, which covers and shields you from exposure, injury, damage, and destruction. Your enemies cannot penetrate the sturdy walls of God's tent. Its firm foundation has been in place for thousands of years. Psalm 27:5-6 explains how God's tent offers protection: "For in the day of trouble He will hide me in his shelter; in the secret place of His tent will He hide me; He will set me high upon a rock. And now my head will be lifted up above my enemies around me, in His tent I will offer sacrifices with shouts of joy; I will sing, yes, I will sing praises to the LORD" (AMPC).

Double underline the three promises God will do to protect you in your day(s) of trouble. Highlight how you should respond.

Who lifts your head above your enemies?

Describe what it means to know He hides *you* in the secret place of his tent.

SPIRITUALLY DEEP WATERS

Some, like Cindie [F], stake their tent in God's refuge and protection years before they face any struggles. A breast cancer diagnosis shocked her; she was otherwise healthy. The words *disease, treatment,* and *dying* penetrated her every thought. Her husband offered comfort, which eased her fears. She knew protection and refuge would be found when she continued to seek shelter in God's tent.

A wise friend shared some wisdom with Cindie. Her friend's words challenged her to consider not only what she could lose, but also what she could gain, during this challenge. She said, "Without adversity, you swim in spiritually shallow waters." Chemo, double mastectomy, radiation, and reconstruction surgery within a year plunged Cindie into spiritually deep waters. Was she going to sink or swim?

The enemy whispered lies about her impending death, her kids growing up without her, how she would experience excruciating pain, and the number of years she would fight this disease. This unexpected turn had her running straight into God's tent, where she refuted those lies by speaking out loud what God's Word said about her. Conversations with God helped her navigate the unknowns ahead of her.

She recovered from double mastectomy surgery and scars began to form. Cindie appreciated how she'd been tossed in waters way over her head, but with God's help, she was swimming stronger than ever before. During her interview, she said, "I realized I had never fully trusted God. My family and I decided to trust God, and it grew our faith. I learned I never had control of my life. I had to make a daily decision to let God be in control. When we did that, we experienced His peace." Those deep waters strengthened Cindie's faith.

Five years after her diagnosis, *remission* is the word Cindie professes every time she shares her story. She takes advantage of every opportunity to encourage and support women who have been given a breast cancer diagnosis, always pointing them to the importance of choosing to reside in God's tent. Additionally, Cindie enjoys working with and teaching students who have dyslexia.

GOD'S TENT OFFERS A PLACE TO REST

Most of us would admit our day-to-day responsibilities exhaust us. Add in caring for an aging parent, or stretching every dollar to pay the bills, or parenting a rebellious teenager, or enduring painful treatments every two weeks. Weariness takes over. Yes, an extra set of hands would be helpful. But what we really need is a place to rest a while. God's tent offers a place to rest, recover, and renew.

When your struggles drag you through the mud, cause resistance and opposition at every turn, God opens the door of His tent and invites you to rest. Your physical body needs rest. Your brain that has been spinning at ninety miles an hour needs rest. Your strung-out and stomped-on emotions need rest. He offers you rest in Matthew 11:28: "Come to me, all you who are weary and burdened, and I will give you rest." Maybe you'd like to accept Jesus's offer to rest but juggling your work and family responsibilities along with the demands of your struggle doesn't leave much room for it. It could be that even if you made time to rest, you don't know how to rest.

During one of the many years of my unrelenting fatigue, I took a class at a speaker's conference with the author of *Sacred Rest*, Dr. Saundra Dalton-Smith. After hearing her patients' concerns for years about how they consistently felt exhausted, she began studying rest to determine why extra sleeping did little to refresh them. She discovered, "Sleep is solely a physical activity. Rest, however, penetrates into the spiritual. Rest speaks peace into the daily storms your mind, body, and spirit encounter."[4] Ah ... We need sleep *and* rest when we are facing storms. So instead of just one type of rest (sleep), she determined there are seven types of rest — physical, mental, emotional, spiritual, social, sensory, and creative. Dr. Dalton-Smith began prescribing rest in those seven areas, pointing out, "The most effective rest occurs when we are purposefully reviving the parts of our life we regularly deplete."[5] Those patients who followed her prescription of resting in their depleted areas were incredible. Consistently taking time to rest improved their health and their mindset, especially when facing life's tough challenges.

Extra sleep is often what we resort to when we finally give in and rest. For some, that extra sleep provides the boost they needed while others wake up groggy, irritable, and still exhausted. As Dr. Dalton-Smith discovered, extra sleep isn't the only type of rest our bodies need. During a season of struggle, your brain is working overtime, so rest must include resting your brain and emotions. Activities that allow you to lose track of time, such as reading, putting jigsaw puzzles together, playing an instrument, painting/drawing/sculpture, or exercising allow your brain to rest, refresh, and renew. Spending time in God's creation connects you to God and offers a healthy dose of vitamin D.

Time with friends who listen, encourage, and pray for you may not seem restful, but feeling cared for and strengthened gives your emotions the rest they need. Taking a break from technology also may not feel like resting, but a constant stream of news often adds to our negative thoughts and feelings. Social media tricks you into believing your friends are *living their best lives* while you're going through a dark time. Their gorgeous pictures and beautiful posts almost convince you that your friends couldn't be struggling too. It's the social media trap. And you need a break from it.

Your body, brain, and emotions need extra rest when you are going through a tough season. The examples I shared might or might not invite rest for you. If they don't, take some time to think about activities that nourish you. Then schedule time to do them.

Describe how you are resting in God's tent.

OUR EARTHLY TENT

Sometimes, our earthly tent is so ravaged with disease, we experience death before we are ready, which was the case with Tracy. [G] At age forty-two, a stage 4 stomach cancer diagnosis was an unexpected turn in her journey. It changed her life dramatically. After spending time in God's tent, she knew how God wanted her to navigate this new path. Tracy met this rare and aggressive form of cancer with a proclamation: "I feel like I have two purposes: I'm going through this to bring glory to God. It's all about Him; and to show my precious children what it's like to walk to hell and back with a strong faith." Courage and strength filled Tracy, empowering her to fight to overcome.

In a discussion about the prognosis for her type of cancer, her oncologist shared, "The survival rate for your cancer is 4%." That dismal number compelled Tracy to consider a radical surgical procedure, which could increase her survival rate to 27%. When Tracy made the decision to have the radical surgery, her family joined her in praying for a successful outcome. Her eight-year-old daughter, Leah, made a poster to remind her of who was fighting stomach cancer with her. It read, "Nothing is impossible with God!"

Just a few short months after learning she had stomach cancer, she underwent a radical twelve-hour gastrectomy to remove her entire stomach. Her surgeon then attached her esophagus to her small intestine. He removed more than twenty-five cancerous lymph nodes and then added a heated chemo wash to cleanse her entire abdominal cavity with the hope of completely ridding her body of cancer.

LIVING LIFE TO THE FULLEST

During the first few weeks after surgery, intense pain invaded her weak body. Some would have thrown up their hands. Tracy didn't. She kept fighting to overcome. She believed the surgery increased her life expectancy. Living this new life to the fullest—thriving despite the challenges— became her mission. Mission impossible? Maybe. Injecting laughter into every conversation and checking items off her bucket list fueled her mission. One of the items she joyfully checked off her bucket list was remarrying Jack, the man who stole her heart many years ago and the father of their three children.

A re-occurrence of stomach cancer appeared a few months after her three-year surgery anniversary. She underwent two surgeries to stop the spread of the cancer, but a third re-occurrence happened despite her surgeon's best efforts. Tracy passed away three months shy of her four-year surgery anniversary. When reviewing this snippet of Tracy's story, Jack asked that I share this about Tracy: "Even though God did not answer specific prayers for Tracy's physical healing, He used the whole experience for His glory. He used her pain and suffering to show His love and power despite her physical circumstances. Tracy's perseverance and hope impacted, encouraged, and inspired those who knew her."

A HOUSE NOT MADE WITH HANDS

Tracy left this earth knowing she would gain an eternal tent that far outshone her cancer-ridden body. She believed in the promises found in 2 Corinthians 5:1-4:

> "For we know that if the earthly tent [our physical body] which is our house is torn down [through death], we have a building from God, a house not made with hands, eternal in the heavens. For indeed in this house, we groan, longing to be clothed with our [immortal, eternal] celestial dwelling, so that by putting it on we will not be found naked. For while we are in this tent, we groan, being burdened [often weighed down, oppressed], not that we want to be unclothed [separated by death from the body], but to be clothed, so that what is mortal [the body] will be swallowed up by life [after the resurrection]" (AMPC).

Our earthly tent *will* crumble and die. We know this intellectually, but we push that knowledge to the back of our minds, thinking we will deal with it later. Tomorrow is not promised. Your earthly tent could crumble and die forty years from now, or it could happen tomorrow. Are you ready?

Spend a moment considering the following question: Are you confident that when your earthly tent gives way to death, you will be clothed in an immortal, eternal, celestial body? Journal your thoughts.

You may feel this chapter is ending on a gloomy note. But sunshine abounds when we remember we have God's protection/refuge and a safe place to rest while living in our earthly tents. It shines even brighter on the wonderful news that one day in the future we will gain a heavenly tent. Pack up your tent, friend, so we can keep moving forward.

> There is something you can't fix, can't heal, or can't escape, and all you can do is trust God. Finding ultimate refuge in God means you become so immersed in His Presence, so convinced of His goodness, so devoted to His Lordship that you find even the cave is a perfectly safe place to be because He is there.6
> —Author and pastor John Ortberg

mile 04

Who Is Guiding Your Journey?

> The Word of God is a treasure map. That treasure map is the most valuable thing you have until you get to that treasure.1
> —Eric Ludy, author and pastor

The days of spreading out a map on the kitchen table and planning an adventure are long gone. We simply type in our destination, and the GPS on our phone or car dashboard directs us there. I love the convenience and lack of planning the GPS map provides. Most of us do! Using a paper map, however, requires planning. Ugghhh. Who has time to plan?!?

A paper map will accurately take you to your destination, but it doesn't provide options for three different routes with approximate times of arrival. Nor can a paper map alert you about heavy traffic and suggest a re-route. Once you're in route to your destination, the paper map would not announce a right turn in three-fourths of a mile. Both types of maps will guide you to your destination. But oh, how wonderful to have access to technology that saves planning time and talks to you! I wonder though, if your GPS quit working, would you be able to reach your destination using a paper map?

If you have terrible map skills, you don't need to worry! We won't be relying on a paper map, or your phone's GPS during our journey. A Bible is the map we will use to guide us, helping you navigate through the challenges impeding your path. The visual image of a map will remind us to seek direction from God's Word, whether we are facing life's toughest struggles or soaking in those carefree sun-shiny days.

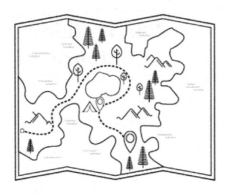

ROAD TRIP

The summer our sons, Ashton and Palmer, were ten and seven respectively, I proposed we take a road trip from our home in Atlanta to New York City. The boys were over the top excited. Jeff wanted to join us, but he could not take that many days of vacation. Given my history of falling dead asleep on the 45-minute drive to my in-law's house, Jeff expressed concern about me being the sole driver on what could be a seven-to-ten-day trip. He begged me to buy plane tickets. I refused. I wanted the boys and I to experience the unknown adventures on the way. "We could explore battlefields in Virginia or the historical monuments in Philadelphia. We can't experience those from an airplane," I pleaded.

Once he relented, I purchased a paper map of the eastern United States. Jeff and I spread it out on the kitchen table and invited the boys to help us plan. I can still see them huddled around Jeff as his finger traced what would be the blue GPS line between Atlanta and New York City. Their excitement built as Jeff described how they could watch movies and listen to books on CD while Mom navigated. The day before we left, he squatted down so he could look the boys in the eye. He said, "Mom can't do this alone. She'll need your help reading the map. And be sure to talk to her to keep her focused on the road." What he meant was, keep her awake.

Each night at the hotel, the boys and I pulled out the paper map and highlighted the stretch of interstate we'd driven that day. Then, we'd talk about what we wanted to explore the next day. This trip occurred before GPS navigation was available in cars, so our paper map was *our only guide* as we headed toward states I'd never visited before. Over the course of ten days, we logged 2,000+ miles and traveled through ten states.

Jeff wrapped us in his arms at the end of those ten days. When we slipped into bed that night, he said, "I'm so proud of you, baby. There were times I was worried about you driving so many hours without another driver to help. But I'm most impressed by your awesome map skills!" While I was proud of myself, the credit belonged to my dad who insisted I learn how to read and use a map.

I could have embarked on our journey without a map, free wheelin' it as I drove. I could have, but I didn't, because I knew I would get lost. I knew frustration, and maybe even panic, would fill me. I knew when I finally figured out the correct roads to take, I would waste time backtracking. I knew taking a journey to an unfamiliar place without a map was unwise.

RELINQUISH THE BELIEF

Your journey matters. How you live the years of your journey matters. You've got no time for free wheelin'. Wasting time getting lost is not on your agenda. You aim to take the right path. Therefore, a reliable and accurate map is essential. Because you haven't traveled this way before, a knowledgeable and experienced guide is a must.

When you pick up your Bible, you're holding THE most reliable and accurate map. It won't guide you onto dark paths, nor will it lead you to dead ends. Quite the opposite. This map invites you to follow the blue line, which zigzagged through the history of God's people. You'll see God at every turn, imparting wisdom and guidance. Trail signs mark the paths of men and women who encountered unexpected turns: vast armies, plagues, betrayal, disappointment, giants, loss, and disease, just to name a few. You'll discover how each of these men and women chose to fight to overcome and the invaluable understanding and insight each gained during their struggles. What each gained during their struggles is offered to you, but you must take it and apply it in your situation. Still uncertain which way to go? The LORD promises, "Whether you turn to the right or to the left, your ears will hear a voice behind you saying, 'This is the way; walk in it'" (Isaiah 30:21). Are you hearing His voice directing your path? God doesn't guide with an audible voice. He speaks to your heart. Lean into Him; He desires for you to hear His voice.

God is a master navigator. He is far more knowledgeable and experienced in navigating tough challenges than any human. God desires to navigate—to make one's way over or through; to steer or manage; to operate or control the course of—your path. Sounds good, doesn't it? Yes, it does ... until we realize we must relinquish the belief *we* are responsible for making, steering, managing, and controlling the course of our path. Ouch, did I step on your toes? My toes are bruised, too. To make progress, you must step aside and invite Him to lead. He is knowledgeable about the rocky terrain you're encountering, as well as what is ahead on your path. His expansive experience with navigating others through their tough challenges is assurance He can navigate you through yours too. Oh, how freeing it is when He is leading and navigating!

Have you relinquished the belief that you are responsible for navigating through your challenge?

Spend a moment thanking God for His map and His expert navigational skills.

PILGRIMS ON THE SAME JOURNEY

Author Nelson DeMille wrote, "We're all pilgrims on the same journey but some pilgrims have better road maps."[2] He isn't referring to the colonists at Plymouth in 1620. Instead, pilgrims are those who journey in foreign lands and are those who encounter unexpected turns.

May I ask you, pilgrim, who or what is guiding you in this foreign land/through this unexpected turn? DeMille suggested something you might not have considered. He said, "the best pilgrims have better road maps." If there are better road maps, then that leads to the possibility that there are some 'not so good' road maps.

A MULTITUDE OF MAPS

No matter the foreign land you find yourself in or the unexpected turn that invaded your journey, a multitude of maps are available to you. Each of those maps promising to guide you. Some are better maps while others are not so good. A few of the more recognizable 'not so good' maps are:

- A map called **culture** lures one into doing "what feels right" or "what makes one happy." This kind of guidance could easily tangle—or further entangle—one in sin, inflict pain on others, and/or cause or add to financial struggles.
- A map called **substances** entices one to numb his/her pain instead of working through it. This kind of guidance often leads to addiction, destroys relationships, and/or leads to job loss.

- A map called **pride** encourages one to cover up or deny a sin or struggle while pushing people who care away because the sin or struggle is perceived as not a big deal or embarrassing. This kind of guidance could destroy a marriage or friendships, cause the loss of a job or ministry, and/or ruin a reputation.

What other 'not so good maps' have tried to entice or lure you in? Describe the all too likely outcomes of their guidance.

FOLLOW THE LIFE-MAP ABSOLUTELY

Allowing these kinds of maps to guide you is a 'not so good' plan. The outcomes you will likely face are 'not so good' either. Let's pull off for a short rest and snack. While we're here, let's look at an invaluable story about maps. King David, as he was about to die, instructed his son, Solomon, to rely on God's map to navigate his life.

As you read 1 Kings 2:13, underline the six instructions King David gave Solomon.

> "When David's time to die approached, he charged his son Solomon, saying, 'I'm about to go the way of all the earth, but you—be strong; show what you're made of! Do what God tells you. Walk in the paths he shows you: Follow the life-map absolutely, keep an eye out for the

signposts, his course for life set out in the revelation to Moses; then you'll get on well in whatever you do and wherever you go'" (MSG).

Now, write the instructions below.

1.
2.
3.
4.
5.
6.

Write the outcome David promised Solomon if he followed those instructions.

A little backstory will remind us why this moment held more importance than just passing the royal baton. When Solomon was a young boy, King David made God's Word part of his daily life, making sure he knew God's commandments. King David's charge to Solomon when he was on his deathbed was direct: follow the life-map absolutely. He didn't say kind of follow it, nor did he say follow it when you feel like it.

Upon inheriting the throne, Solomon chose to follow his father's charge, worshiping and offering burnt sacrifices to God in Gibeon. While there, God appeared to him in a dream and said, "What can I give you? Ask" (1 Kings 3:5).

Highlight the question God asked Solomon. Describe the thoughts and emotions you would have if God asked you that question. How would you reply?

In 1 Kings 3:9, Solomon replied, "Here's what I want: Give me a God-listening heart so I can lead your people well, discerning the difference between good and evil. For who on their own is capable of leading your glorious people?"

In the verse above, underline what Solomon wanted. Highlight 'For who on their own is capable of leading your glorious people.'

Can you imagine God's delight upon hearing Solomon's response? God replied, "Because you have asked for this and haven't grasped after a long life, or riches, or the doom of your enemies, but you have asked for the ability to lead and govern well, I'll give you what you asked for—I'm giving you a wise and mature heart. There's 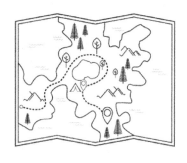 never been one like you before; and there'll be no one after. As a bonus, I'm giving you both the wealth and glory you didn't ask for – there's not a king anywhere who will come up to your mark. And if you stay on course, keeping your eye on the life-map and the God-signs as your father David did, I'll also give you long life" (1 Kings 3:10-14, MSG).

God's response to Solomon was far more than he asked for. Underline and then record the six things God promised to give Solomon.

1.
2.
3.
4.
5.
6.

Write the one condition Solomon must meet to receive a long life.

SEDUCED HIM AWAY FROM GOD

The seventh condition—a long life—would be given *if* Solomon continued to keep his eye on the life-map and the God-signs. A long life was conditional, not guaranteed. King Solomon took to heart what God said to him. He put Godly men in leadership positions. He finished rebuilding the Temple his father started and dedicated it to God. He offered burnt sacrifices. He led his people in prayers, pointing them to God. He consistently sought God's guidance. Solomon was serious about following God's life-map.

Until ... we get to chapter 11 of First Kings. Solomon started following a different map—one that guided him to the 'not so good' ways of the world's tent. Look at 1 Kings 11:1-11:

"King Solomon was obsessed with women. Pharaoh's daughter was only the first of the many foreign women he loved—Moabite, Ammonite, Edomite, Sidonian, and Hittite. He took them from the surrounding pagan nations of which God had clearly warned Israel, 'You must not marry them, they'll seduce you with infatuations with their gods.' Solomon fell in love with many of those women anyway, refusing to give them up. He had seven hundred royal wives and three hundred concubines—a thousand women in all. And they seduced him away from God, just as God said they would. As Solomon grew older, his wives beguiled him with their alien gods, and he became unfaithful. He didn't stay true to his God as his father David had done. Solomon took up with Ashtoreth, the whore goddess of the Sidonians, and Molech, the horrible god of the Ammonites. Solomon openly defied God; he did not follow in his father David's footsteps. He went on to

build a sacred shrine to Chemosh, the horrible god of Moab, and to Molech, the horrible god of the Ammonites, on a hill just east of Jerusalem. He built similar shrines for all his foreign wives, who then polluted the countryside with the smoke and stench of their sacrifices" (MSG).

LED TO HIS DESTRUCTION

Wow! Solomon's shoved aside his God-map and chose to follow the map of lust. Willfully being led astray by ungodly influences was the map that took him off course. While some turns are truly unexpected, other turns are taken by choice. Those turns often lead to dangerous outcomes. Solomon chose to follow the map of idolatry, putting other gods before the one true God. That map ultimately led to his destruction. How did God react to Solomon's choices?

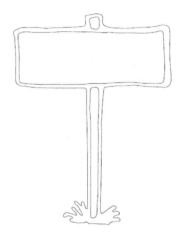

As you read 1 Kings 11:10-13, highlight what God ripped away from Solomon.

"God was furious with Solomon for abandoning the God of Israel, the God who had twice appeared to him and had so clearly commanded him not to fool around with other gods. Solomon faithlessly disobeyed God's orders. God said to Solomon, 'Since this is the way it is with you, that you have no intention of keeping faith with me and doing what I have commanded, I'm going to rip the kingdom from you and hand it over to someone else. But out of respect for your father David I won't do it in your lifetime. It's your son who will pay—I'll rip it right out of his grasp. Even then I won't take it all; I'll leave him one tribe in

honor of my servant David and out of respect for my chosen city Jerusalem."

Ripping is not a polite action. It means "to tear, split, or open something quickly or violently." Solomon not only had access to a God map, but he also had a direct line of communication with the Master navigator: God. He decided he didn't need his God-map or his God. Because Solomon chose to follow an ungodly map, he suffered quick and violent consequences. And sadly, so did his son. God promised to give Solomon's son, Rehoboam, the kingdom when Solomon died. All but one tribe of Israel was stripped away from Rehoboam. Additionally, God incited adversaries against Solomon's kingdom. Trouble heaped on trouble. In those days, passing away at eighty was not considered a long life. As promised, God ripped away his opportunity to live a long life, too.

Solomon suffered greatly because he chose to follow other maps. In the space below, describe why God's Word is a better map to follow.

BELIEVED GOD WOULD HEAL

Wanda [H] knows the power of following God's map and speaking His Word over the struggles in her life. When her husband, Jerry, was diagnosed with throat cancer, she didn't panic. Cancer was an unexpected turn, but she knew following God's word—the best directional guide—would point them in the right direction. Because healing was the destination she desired, she looked up verses on healing. She spoke those verses out loud every single day, which strengthened her faith, trusting that God could and would heal her husband.

Chemotherapy and radiation treatments led to Jerry's healing. Almost three years later, Wanda began having symptoms like those Jerry experienced. Testing showed she too had throat cancer, although it was a different strain of the virus Jerry had. Surgery wasn't possible as the tumor was pushing against her carotid artery.

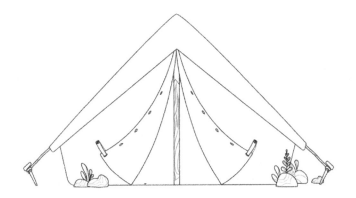

Wanda quickly found her healing verses. "I remembered how saying and believing those verses healed Jerry. His healing led me to truly trusting God. So, I took my health issues to Him right from the beginning." Her response to the chemotherapy and radiation treatments didn't go as smoothly as Jerry's. In frustration, she retreated to God's tent and pleaded, "I can't do this anymore, God. My healing is manifested or take me home."

God listened and answered. Further treatments led to her healing. Passing the five-year mark signified her remission. You won't find this spunky lady couch surfing. Instead, she's pumping iron at the gym, enjoying adventures with Jerry, making quilts for loved ones, and treasuring every second with her son's family, which includes a great granddaughter. A daily dedication to seeking God's guidance in His Word is a priority as she continues heading toward her eternal destination.

MOST VALUABLE TREASURE MAP

If you have God's map, are you using it? Or is it on your bookshelf, gathering dust? If it's on your bookshelf gathering dust, you're missing out on all the ways it can help you navigate life and any tough struggle in your path. In the opening quote for this mile of our journey, Eric Ludy said, "The Word of God is a treasure map."

Does God command we read/study His Word daily? No, but King David did. He believed God's Word was a treasure map. One he wanted to study and to guide him. He eagerly studied because he'd experienced the benefits of studying it at the beginning of his day: "Let the morning bring me word of your unfailing love, for I have put my trust in you. Show me the way I should go, for to you I entrust my life" (Psalm 143:8).

In the passage above, highlight the two requests David makes of God.

Describe how God, answering those two requests, led David to putting his trust in God and entrusting God with his life.

Ludy also said, "The treasure map is the most valuable thing we have until you get to that treasure." Every step of your journey is meant to lead you to the most valuable treasure. By listening to the Master navigator's voice and following His map, He is steering you to the ultimate destination—the most valuable treasure—heaven.

GUIDES US TOWARD OUR ETERNAL DESTINATION

Along our journey, we will accumulate a few bumps and bruises, even a scar or two. We know those are part of fighting to overcome our struggles. Thankfully, our journey won't only be comprised of challenges. God will also fill our path with joy, adventure, peace, love, and friendship.

As if His guidance while we are here on earth wasn't enough, God's map serves another purpose. An even better purpose! His Word guides us toward our eternal destination: the treasure called heaven. Despite the 622 references to heaven in God's Word, our eternal destination remains a mysterious place.

Before we move onto mile 05, let's study our map by looking up a few verses. As you read the following verses, allow the Master Navigator to describe what's ahead when we reach our eternal destination.

- We will have eternal life. (John 6:40)
- Our bodies will be transformed. (Philippians 3:20-21)
- We are heirs of God and co-heirs with Christ. (Romans 8:17)
- We will receive an inheritance. (Colossians 3:24)
- We will see God's face and reign with Him. (Revelation 22:4-5)

A promise about what lies ahead is found in 1 Corinthians 2:7-9:

> *"But rather what we are setting forth is a wisdom of God once hidden [from the human understanding] and now revealed to us by God—[that wisdom] which God devised and decreed before the ages for our glorification [to lift us into the glory of His presence]. None of the rulers of this age or world perceived and recognized and understood this, for if they had, they would never have crucified the Lord of glory. But, on the contrary, as the Scripture says, 'What eye has not seen and ear has not heard and has not entered into the heart of man, [all that] God has prepared (made and keeps ready) for those who love Him [who hold Him in affectionate reverence, promptly obeying Him and gratefully recognizing the benefits He has bestowed]'"* (AMPC).

WOW! Take a moment to meditate on those promise filled words! Does it excite you to know God has already prepared things for you that are so amazing your physical senses can't contain it? Let's get going! Each piece of gear in the miles ahead are equally as beneficial and helpful for your journey.

> A Bible that's falling apart usually belongs to someone who isn't.3
> —English preacher and theologian, Charles H. Spurgeon

mile 05

Who Do You Call on When You're Struggling?

There are parts of our calling, works of the Holy Spirit, and defeats of the darkness that will come no other way than through furious, fervent, faith-filled, unceasing prayer.1

—Beth Moore, author and Bible teacher

You might be thinking the gear we've packed thus far has been a bit predictable. It's common sense to pack a tent and a map for an extended journey, right? Maybe. Maybe not. As they say, "Common sense isn't so common anymore." Choosing God's tent instead of the world's tent may feel limiting and restrictive to some, but not to us. We know God's tent promises unlimited and unrestricted protection, refuge, and rest. And as we know from experience, there is a daily invitation to follow the world's maps. We've learned those maps guide people toward sin, destruction, and pain. We've chosen to follow God's map instead because we know His guidance will lead us toward abundant life, restoration, and joy.

Sometimes, we've firmly staked our lives in God's tent and are following His map, but something still isn't connecting. This disconnected feeling frightens us, so we share our concerns with a spouse or friend. We need to express, process, and unravel our difficult struggle. However, the time it would take to describe our feelings and frustrations would be akin to traveling the full 2,340 miles of the Mississippi River, not to mention the patience needed if we took a tangent down one of its 250 tributaries. Maybe you don't take tangents when sharing your feelings, but I definitely do. I love my man and my friends, but none of them have that kind of time or patience. Besides, no human can provide the answers or the healing or the peace that God can provide. Not only does God have the time and patience to listen to us, but He is also the only one who can give the answers we are so desperate for while providing the deep connection our hearts long for.

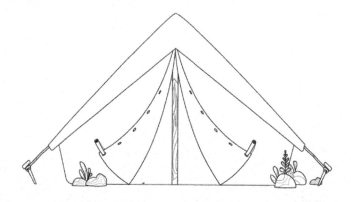

When you chat with someone other than God about your struggle, does he or she respond by asking, "What are you going to do?"

In the space below, describe how that question makes you feel.

I despise that question. I've already been asking myself that question, and not having an answer stresses me out. That question increases my anxiety and fear. I invariably begin imagining every worst-case scenario instead of believing God wants the best for me. When I share my concerns with God, He never asks me what I'm going to do. He knows I don't know what to do. By sharing with Him, instead of my husband or a friend, I put figuring out what to do in His hands—His capable hands. Praying doesn't add to my stress, fears, or anxiety. In fact, it significantly lessens those negative and destructive emotions.

PURPOSES OF PRAYER

Prayer serves a multitude of purposes. Is there a piece of gear that could represent this amazing blessing God gives us? Indeed, there is! A multi-purpose tool serves multiple purposes and is an essential tool to carry with you on your journey.

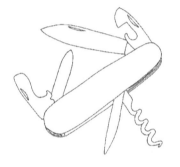

Check out a few purposes that are fulfilled when a hiker uses a multi-tool: Need a hook disgorger to remove a hook from your dinner's mouth? Need a can opener to open a can of beans to pair with your fish? How about tweezers to remove a splinter from the wood you chopped for the fire? A multi-tool handles each of these with ease. Remember Swiss Army knives? Because prayer, like a multi-purpose tool, provides numerous ways to help and support us while on our journey, the visual image of a multi-purpose tool will represent prayer.

When you seek God in prayer, His purposes are fulfilled in your life. Be assured God won't tap his foot or glance at His watch, sending you signals to hurry it up. His time and patience are inexhaustible. The multiple purposes of prayer are too many to cover each one here, but let's look at a few.

1. Prayer connects you with the only One who truly knows you. The Creator of the universe created your inmost being. He knit you together in your mother's womb (Psalm 139:13). God knows you inside and out because He created you. He, better than any human, knows and understands your struggles, frustrations, insecurities, and pain. When you connect with Him in prayer, you are building and maintaining a deep connection with your heavenly Father.

2. Prayer invites a two-way connection with the One who hears your words *and* your heart: "You will call on me and come and pray to me, and I will listen to you. You seek me and find me when you seek me with all your heart" (Jeremiah 29:12-13). Not only does He hear you, but He also answers: "Hear my prayer, LORD; listen to my cry for mercy. When I am in distress, I call to you, because you answer me" (Psalm 86: 6-7). The most beautiful aspect of this two-way connection with God is that He is always available. At three in the morning when worry keeps you from sleeping? Yep, He's available. When friends no longer take your calls because they are tired of hearing about your struggles? Even then. Especially then. Call out to Him instead. He longs to have conversations with you.

3. Prayer strengthens you. When fears cripple, enemies attack, and challenges overwhelm, you can cry out to God for help. Not only does He walk right beside you, but He also strengthens you. Cling to this promise when you feel weak: "Do not fear, for I am with you; do not be dismayed, for I am your God. I will strengthen you and help you; I will uphold you with my righteous right hand" (Isaiah 41:10).

4. Prayer guides your path. Just as studying God's map directs your path, so does prayer. Perhaps you study His map, but you're still confused about which path to take. Ask Him for guidance and wisdom. He is eager to direct or redirect you to the right path. King David didn't earn the reputation as a skilled and wise military leader on his own accord. He gained those skills because he prayed: "Show me your ways, LORD, teach me your paths. Guide me in your truth and teach me, for you are God my Savior, and my hope is in you all day long" (Psalm 25:4-5).

5. Prayer fills you with a peace that passes (human) understanding. The enemy is strategic. He knows if he can steal your peace that the suffocating anxiety, worry, and fear you feel will weaken you tremendously. This added chaos leaves you vulnerable and an easy target for further attacks. But when you pray, God fills you with peace, which is the enemy's Kryptonite. Consider Philippians 4:6-7: "Do not be anxious about anything, but in every situation, by prayer and petition, with thanksgiving, present your requests to God. And the peace of God, which transcends all understanding, will guard your hearts and your minds in Christ Jesus." Let the peace you feel assure you that God is working.

6. Prayer allows God to impart His insight, wisdom and understanding. Likely, you've seen how misguided and misdirected the world's insight, wisdom, and understanding are. Only one source provides true and trustworthy insight, wisdom, and understanding. God imparts what you need to be strong and courageous, not give up, and fight to overcome the struggles in your path. May King Solomon's words encourage you to seek God in prayer.

As you read the following verses from Proverbs 2, highlight the benefits of inviting God to impart His insight, wisdom, and understanding.

> My son, if you accept my words and store up my commands within you, turning your ear to wisdom and applying your heart to understanding—indeed, if you call out for insight and cry aloud for understanding, and if you look for it as for silver and search for it as for hidden treasure, then you will understand the fear of the LORD and find the knowledge of God. For the LORD gives wisdom; from his mouth come knowledge and understanding. He holds success in store for the upright, he is a shield to those whose walk is blameless, for he guards the course of the just and protects the way of his faithful ones. Then you will understand what is right and just and fair—every good path. For wisdom will enter your heart, and knowledge will be pleasant to your soul. Discretion will protect you, and understanding will guard you (Proverbs 2:1-11).

7. Prayer offers thanks to God. Even when your world is in shambles, evidence of God's love, kindness, and mercy are everywhere. Take a moment to "see" them and then offer thanks. Maybe a friend visited you after surgery, or a sunset calmed your frazzled nerves. Perhaps an unexpected bonus was added to your paycheck, or you shared a hot mug of coffee with a loved one. Each of these examples, and a million more, invite you and I to offer thanksgiving to God. Express your thanks in prayer or say it out loud. Paul describes when to offer thanks: "Rejoice always, pray continually, give thanks in all circumstances; for this is God's will for you in Christ Jesus." Yes, give thanks in *all* circumstances!" (1 Thessalonians 5:16-18)

What other purposes of prayer have you experienced?

Describe specific instances when prayer impacted you in a powerful way.

PRAYER WARRIOR

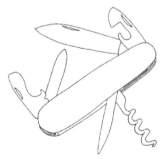

My father-in-law, Wayne¹, was a prayer warrior. He believed in Romans 12:12: "Be joyful in hope, patient in affliction, faithful in prayer." Because prayer impacted him numerous times throughout his life, he knew every situation—big or small—could be taken to God in prayer.

Nine blockages in Wayne's heart took him by surprise. He felt poorly for weeks, but his doctors couldn't find anything wrong with him. Finally, a heart catheterization revealed blockages in his heart. When we visited him after his five-by-pass heart surgery, he was eager to share what he was learning through prayer. While he prayed for healing, he also prayed his fear of the unknown and death would not be bigger than his faith. He knew Ralph Waldo Emerson's words were true: "The wise man in the storm prays not for safety from danger but for deliverance from fear."[2]

Just as the scar on his chest was beginning to lighten, a planned colonoscopy caused an unexpected turn in Wayne's journey. More tests were ordered. A bone marrow biopsy revealed a very low white blood cell count. A diagnosis of myelodysplastic syndrome, a precursor to cancer, was given. Despite treatments, a diagnosis of acute myeloid leukemia (AML) followed. Frustrated but not defeated, Wayne reached for his multi-purpose tool.  Conversations with God were his lifeline. Prayer sustained him during the multiple-day nose bleeds, numerous blood transfusions, and chemo treatments. Intense pain, a lack of stamina, and the unrelenting fatigue would have been unbearable if not for his multi-purpose tool. Prayer was his on-going connection with God, and it strengthened him. Communicating with God through prayer helped him navigate his difficult journey. Peace replaced his fear of death, especially on the days leading up to his passing.

Wayne surpassed the dismal six-month prognosis by an additional twelve months. He bravely fought until his very last breath. Wayne's faith became impenetrable because of his determination to dwell in God's tent, study God's map, and rely on his multi-purpose tool of prayer. While it saddened his family when his earthly tent was torn down, we are confident Wayne is living in his eternal home with God.

NOISE IN OUR LIVES

I wonder if you, like me, have diligently sought God in prayer and experienced a deafening silence. A response of 'no' would be easier to accept than God's silence. Frustration sets in. Maybe even an obstinate, arms crossed posture. Perhaps you've quit praying as prayer seems futile. May I suggest that sometimes He answers, but we don't hear it? Sometimes the noise in our lives prevents us from hearing His voice. Distractions that fill your eyes and occupy your thoughts are noise. If you want to hear God's voice, you need to minimize or eliminate distractions on a regular basis. You don't want to miss hearing God's voice.

In the space below, list the noise(s) in your life: those things that distract you from hearing God's voice. For each *noise* you listed, describe a way to reduce that noise. Commit to implementing those changes.

QUIET DURING A TEST

Maybe you have eliminated as much of the noise from your life as humanly possible, but you're still not hearing God's answer to your prayers.

Meditate on this quote: "When you're going through something hard and wonder where God is, remember the teacher is always quiet during a test."[3] What comes to mind when you think about this quote?

Let's consider why teachers—and God—might be quiet during a test. Likely, you remember teachers give tests, so you can demonstrate what you've learned. If a teacher shared answers with you throughout the test, would your grade reflect what you learned? No. Because noise and distractions make retrieving information challenging, your teacher insisted upon a quiet environment. For an academic test, you must demonstrate your knowledge and skills about a unit or semester's worth of information during a specific time frame. Life tests aren't bound by a time frame. Multiple opportunities to learn a lesson may need to occur before you truly understand the concept well enough to pass your life test.

Second, tests are opportunities to assess your growth. Maybe you expressed your confusion in a prayer as the questions are worded differently than how you learned the information. God listened to your plea for help, but He didn't answer. Why not? Life's test questions are rarely a simple recall of information. Remembering and understanding are the two lowest levels on Bloom's Taxonomy of Learning.[4] Instead, life's tests require more of you. God is silent because He's waiting for you to remember and understand the knowledge and skills you've learned from previous life experiences and then apply, analyze, evaluate, and create it in your current situation. Growth is the bridge between remembering/understanding and applying/analyzing/evaluating/creating. He's silent because growth isn't given. It's acquired. You acquire growth by going through challenges, frustrations, pain, and struggles.

Your growth is of utmost importance to God, so while He may be quiet during your life tests, He is not absent. Quite the opposite. Keep praying. He knows what you are facing and longs to connect with you, strengthen you, guide you, fill you with peace, and impart His insight, wisdom, and understanding. You won't see these responses with your eyes, but tune into the quiet, and you'll feel them with your heart. When you do, be sure to thank Him.

Describe a time when God was quiet during one of your tests.

UGLY BEAST OF COMPARISON

Let's continue the student analogy for a moment longer. A distinct look of fear or embarrassment is often seen on a student's face when he is one of the last to finish a test, especially when a friend finished twenty minutes before him and is napping on her desk. No matter how much encouragement a teacher offers, that student feels defeated and stupid. Why? The beast of comparison has reared its ugly head.

This premise is not just limited to school-aged children and their academic tests. We, as mature and intellectually competent adults, do it too with the tests we face in life. Suppose excess spending has become a stronghold in your life. You and a close friend take a financial freedom class. Armed with information, you both

create a budget and a plan for eliminating debt. You check in with each other from time to time. When you learn she is debt-free after two years, you begin to question how that is possible. You have paid off several credit card bills and are making a dent in your mortgage, but you are nowhere near debt-free. How did she finish her test so quickly?

Because most people do not share explicit details about their finances, you had no idea she didn't have to contend with mortgage payments as she inherited her home from her parents. She chose not to spend any money on new clothes during that two-year period, yet God opened a door to your dream job, which required you to update your professional wardrobe. Many other factors could explain why your friend became debt free in two years. We will never understand—nor does God have to explain—why others may experience less challenges when going through a similar test.

In God's classroom, there is no room for comparison. We must believe the tests we are given are designed to grow and strengthen us, as well as build our faith and trust in Him. Never mistake God's silence during your tests. Do not believe the lies that He does not care or is not working. Diligently seek Him. Keep praying, friend.

PUT MY TEARS INTO YOUR BOTTLE

As a child, Rhonda J didn't understand the raging verbal attacks her father directed at her. His demeaning and hurtful words crushed her self-esteem. Unfortunately, it wasn't limited to his words. Beating her with a belt left marks on her hands and arms. His uncontrollable behaviors embarrassed Rhonda, causing her to never invite friends to her home. "I did not *know* God as a child. I *knew of* Him," Rhonda shared. She remembers crying out to God after receiving a Bible and being baptized when she was sixteen. She cried out to God just like David did in Psalm 56:8-9: "You number and record my wanderings; put my tears into Your bottle—are they not in Your book? Then shall my enemies turn back in the day that I cry out; this I know, for God is for me" (AMPC).

On the night of her high school Christmas cello performance, Rhonda's dad was in a rage. She could hear him loading a gun in his bedroom. Realizing what he could be preparing to do, she ran to her friend's apartment, slammed the front door behind her, and ran to the farthest bedroom. "I was terrified." To escape his erratic behavior, she moved to Florida to live with her mom. At the time, it may have felt like God wasn't listening to Rhonda's prayers, but His best for Rhonda was on its way.

Rhonda was flattered to hear a young man named Lloyd wanted to ask her out, but it took months for him to build up the courage. She quickly learned after a few dates that Lloyd was nothing like her father. Her family loved him and encouraged their relationship. Not only did God collect Rhonda's tears of pain from her childhood years, but He also collected her tears of joy as she fell in love with a man who loved God. Three years later, Rhonda and Lloyd were married.

When their daughter was born, Rhonda and Lloyd rejoiced. However, their daughter's behavior became challenging soon after their son, Mitchell, was born. Every plan the school designed to help her learn, she thwarted. Mitchell's behavior was also challenging. "Even as young as two, there was a fire in Mitchell's eyes," Rhonda explained. When Mitchell was in his last year of middle school, he moved into a full-time Christian program with an integrated approach for home, education, counseling, and spiritual life. The counseling and treatment Mitchell received provided healing, both for him and the family.

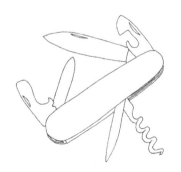

When Rhonda reflected on her life during her interview, she could clearly see that God has been a consistent thread throughout her life. A beautiful tapestry woven with Rhonda's tears of pain and tears of joy. She believes, "The struggles I went through were meant to lead me closer to God. I released all of it to God in prayer. He collected my tears when I cried out to Him, and He worked in the lives of my children, my marriage, and my health. Seeing both of our children as well-rounded and contributing adults gives us peace that the fight was worth it. God was behind all of it!" She and Lloyd enjoy spending time with their adult children and grandchildren. Until it's time to retire, Rhonda works part-time as a dental hygienist.

PRAYER CHANGES YOU

Calling out to God through prayer is by far your best choice when you're in a challenging struggle, or when you feel you've run out of options. Call out to Him when your loneliness is overwhelming. But don't forget that He's also the best choice to call on when you're having the best day ever, or when you're excited about new opportunities. Call out when you're so full of gratitude you can't help but share it with Him. The beautiful thing about prayer is it fulfills many purposes.

Put your multi-purpose tool in an easily accessible place in your backpack. Use it in the morning, throughout the day, and before you close your eyes at night. God loves to hear your heart when you call out to Him.

> Prayer doesn't change God. It changes me.[5]
> —C.S. Lewis, author and theologian

mile 06

Is Darkness Impeding Your Path?

> Now, God be praised, that to believing souls gives light in darkness, comfort in despair.1
> —William Shakespeare, English playwright

When Jeff turns off the lights in our bedroom at night, it's not totally dark. The red glow of my alarm clock cuts through the darkness. Hazy light from the nearby streetlight slips in through the slats, even when the blinds are closed as tightly as possible. A full moon emits a bright glow, softening the dark.

Several years ago, however, the power went out on a night that had just the tiniest sliver of a moon. We could not see more than an inch in front of our faces. Lighting a match dispelled the eerie darkness. Light overcame the darkness.

Creepy back alleys. Deserted roads. An abandoned warehouse at night. The looming darkness encircles you. Uncertainty fills your mind. Fear of the unknown causes your stomach to tighten. Add in an unfamiliar screeching sound, and you're undone. Perhaps you've experienced those kinds of darkness. As scary as that complete darkness is, it's far scarier when that darkness is disrupting or destroying your life. Whatever struggle you are facing, dark is likely a good descriptor. It's nearly impossible to make your way out of the dark without help. The only means of overcoming darkness is light.

If you are in a dark place now, describe it and the feelings it is producing in you.

If you've experienced a dark place and are no longer there, describe how you navigated out of it.

Light dispels darkness and illuminates potential dangers in your path. Roots won't trip you as you'll spot them with your eyes well before your feet find them. Low hanging branches won't knock you in the head or poke out your eyes. Snakes slither away in the opposite direction for fear of being exposed. A flashlight will represent light overcoming the darkness.

THE LIGHT OF ALL MANKIND

The first eighteen verses of the gospel of John describe the attributes of 'a man' who would not be recognized by the world, but "In him was life, and that light was the light of all mankind. The light shines in the darkness, and the darkness has not overcome it" (verses 4-5). John doesn't reveal who 'this man' is but asserts "the true light that gives light to everyone was coming into the world" (verse 9).

Oh, to be in the crowd with those who heard John's words! How many were there whose hearts skipped a beat when John proclaimed this light could overcome (their) darkness? Could it be true? I can almost hear someone call out, "John, who is 'this man' who gives light to everyone?" Another shouts, "When is this light coming?" For those in the crowd who were desperate for light to shine in their darkness, John's words filled them with hope!

We know 'this man' who gives light to everyone is Jesus! In Him is life. He is the light of all mankind. Jesus shines in the darkness, and the darkness has not overcome Him. Do John's words about Jesus fill you with hope? Jesus, as the true light, *will* shine in the darkness that has overtaken your path. And no matter how menacing that darkness is, no matter how much of a bully it is, and no matter how much pain that darkness causes, our true light, Jesus, *will* overcome it.

Say it out loud with me: Jesus SHINES in the darkness. He will overcome any darkness in my life.

To fully appreciate the powerful light source Jesus is, we need to better understand how we find ourselves surrounded in darkness. Darkness *will* intersect our path, but it is not meant to be a permanent obstacle. Let's consider four ways darkness interrupts our path:

- You're dragged into darkness.
- You experience periods of darkness that suffocate.

- Your unexpected health struggles throw you into darkness.
- You invited darkness in.

For this next section, don't just read the text. Please interact with it. Take note of how the overcomers used their flashlights to dispel the darkness.

DRAGGED INTO DARKNESS

Free-will or choice are never offered by those who drag others into darkness. Fear, violence, and pain are the companions of darkness. Shame and humiliation ride its coattails. Please allow me to repeat this: those experiencing this darkness did not choose it. They were dragged there. With threats of brutal harm to themselves or to their loved ones, those hurt in this darkness are stripped of a voice against their oppressors.

We know Satan comes to kill, steal, and destroy. One powerful way he achieves this evil is to drag unwilling victims into his dark lair of abuse. Emotional, physical, and sexual abuse are an oppressive darkness that stems from one wielding power, violence, and control over another. But there is hope. Hope can be found in the only one who offers freedom, heals abused minds, bodies, and wounded souls. The light of God is the only way to expose and destroy this darkness.

AWARE OF THE ABUSE

If there'd been a National Child Abuse Prevention Month when Tammy [K] was four years old, maybe someone would have believed her cries for help and prevented her abusers from dragging her into a horrifying darkness. With a severe alcoholic as a mother and a stepfather addicted to porn, she didn't have a voice at age four to say "NO" to her stepfather's sexual abuse. At age nine, Tammy's mother walked in during a rape but did nothing to help her or stop it.

Her mother's addiction to men and a deep need for love and atten-

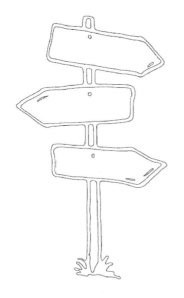

tion influenced her choice to use Tammy as bait to keep men in her life. She knew her mother was aware she was being molested, but instead of shining light into the darkness, Tammy's mother sent her into the darkness again and again. Many men sexually abused Tammy until she ran away from home at sixteen.

Suppressing her memories and deep emotional pain led to a food addiction. By age twenty-six, Tammy weighed over 200 pounds. Three years later, she entered the first of many psychiatric hospitals. Diagnoses of severe depression, anxiety, PTSD, and dissociative identity disorder labeled her pain. During one of her hospital stays, Tammy remembers receiving a heart message from Jesus: *My plans for you are good and do not include you being in mental hospitals for the rest of your life.* Hearing those words fueled her to invite Jesus to heal her. She entered faith-based healing programs, joined many Bible studies, and surrounded herself with a loving Christian community. As she experienced more of Jesus' love, she held tightly to John 12:46: "I have come into the world as a light, so that no one who believes in me should stay in darkness."

OVERCAME THE DARKNESS

It wasn't until Tammy was thirty-five years old that she discovered her mother was keeping a very dark secret. On a Saturday morning just months before her death, Tammy's tearful and very intoxicated mother called her. Between sobs, she begged, "I'm going to hell unless you forgive me!" Her mother admitted receiving money over the years from several of Tammy's abusers. Their phone conversation occurred in 1999 when the term *child trafficking* was not commonly used. Who would believe a mother could allow her child to be raped for years in exchange for money and attention? The darkness Tammy's mother dragged her into could only be overcome by the light of Jesus.

Jesus did overcome that horrifying darkness, healing Tammy of decades of pain, abandonment, shame, and fear. Sharing her story with men, women, and children across the nation who were also dragged into the darkness of sexual abuse, gives her the opportunity to point them to the hope she found in Jesus. Tammy describes  her story of overcoming the darkness in her book, *From Rubble to Royalty*. Since starting her ministry, King's Treasure Box, Tammy has written six books for parents and therapists to read with a child who has been sexually abused. The colorful characters help them discover the truth that what happened to them is not their fault. Learn more at kingstreasurebox.org.

DARKNESS THAT SUFFOCATES

Sometimes darkness threatens to suffocate—to deprive life from; to make uncomfortable by want of fresh air—with an oppressive and unrelenting force. No matter how much she strives to seek the light, darkness demands her attention. Such is the case with invisible, chronic illnesses or mental illnesses. With either of these types of illnesses, a person who diligently seeks light can still feel periods of darkness as she struggles with pain, depression, or the weariness that comes with knowing she might not ever experience complete recovery.

On her stable days, the outside observer may believe a person with a mental illness or chronic illness is no longer struggling, no longer suffocating. They note her smiles and laughter. It's as if she's going about life, unhindered by the oppressive and unrelenting effects of her illness. Because stable days can be far and few between, she takes full advantage of them by interacting with others, enjoying activities, and pursuing her dreams. Often, these days of *living life* are followed by extreme fatigue, irritability, a flare-up, or pain. The darkness once again threatens to suffocate her.

WITHDRAWING FROM LIFE

Diane ᴸ encountered episodes of wild mania and weeks of deep depression for years before the official diagnosis of bipolar disorder was given. Her reckless, bold behavior during her mania episodes may have been thrilling and extremely enjoyable while she was doing them, but the high credit card bills and the trail of hurt feelings embarrassed Diane. Withdrawing from life to sleep, avoiding family and friends, and attempting to take her life several times marked her weeks of suffocating darkness when the depression hit hard.

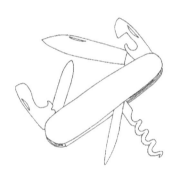

One powerful way she fought and continues to fight when the darkness of her bipolar disorder suffocates her is by grabbing her flashlight. She doubles down on the darkness by studying her map and using her multi-purpose tool. This powerful combination empowers her, so she can continue to fight. Withstanding the high tides of mania and the low tides of depression would be impossible without God's help. She explained, "There are times all I can do is cry out, 'It's all you, Lord. There's nothing I can do myself to get past this. I give it all to you.'"

Each time Diane's mental illness threatens to suffocate her, she shines her flashlight into that pit of darkness. Does it disappear immediately? Not usually. But God's light helps her believe that episode will not destroy her. The light directs her path toward God and away from potentially dangerous and harmful situations. Francis of Assisi's prayer could easily be Diane's prayer when she faces the suffocating darkness: "Great and glorious God, and Thou Lord Jesus, I pray you shed abroad your light in the darkness of my mind. Be found of me, Lord, so that in all things I may act only in accordance with Thy holy will."[2]

In 2020, Diane began compiling years of journal entries that she penned during her darkest days. Rereading those entries reminded her of the periods of time she lived in the suffocating darkness. Thankfully, she also journaled instances when the light of Jesus pierced through that darkness *and* overcame it. Her book, *Journals from a Broken Mind*, encourages readers who suffer from mental illness, reminding them that they are not alone. Diane's words offer hope, that even with a mental illness, living a full and meaningful life is possible.

THROWN INTO DARKNESS

Our bodies break down. Sometimes rogue cells begin attacking healthy cells in our bodies. When our health suffers, it feels like we are rudely thrown into darkness. No one would ask for cancer or a flesh-eating bacteria or gangrene in their leg. When a diagnosis is given and a treatment suggested, we feel the darkness closing in. The enemy jumps in and stirs things up, eagerly watching to see how we process this life-changing news. His darkness fills us with doubt and fear of the unknown. Sometimes we question God for allowing this darkness to invade our lives. When the possibility of death is mentioned, the enemy knows even the best weighted blanket could never calm the anxiety in our hearts.

Can we overcome every disease, cancer, or illness that invades our path? Unfortunately, no. But we can choose—and it is a choice—to shine God's light on the darkness the enemy attaches to the diseases, cancer, or illnesses we face. His bright light shines on the salvation, hope, healing, grace, and mercy He freely gives to us. These powerful gifts from God *will* dispel the darkness.

INVITE DARKNESS IN

For some, living in darkness is exactly where they choose to be. Why would a person choose to invite darkness into her life? Isn't she concerned with the outcomes or consequences? Maybe, but for some, darkness is pleasurable, exciting, and entertaining. Good memories are often made in the dark. Negative consequences might not immediately follow, which reinforces the pull to continue to invite the darkness in.

As much as we might not want to admit it, darkness also offers numbing relief, escape, avoidance of pain, and a shield distancing us from responsibility. Our pressure-filled society and all the expectations put on us might cause the best of us to at least consider the darkness, even poke our toe in it. Believing we can invite the darkness in *just until* the physical, mental, or emotional pain subsides lures us into a trap. Be assured that trap is strategically disguised, but it's a trap, nonetheless. And once we're trapped in its shackles, breaking free is difficult.

CHOSE EXCESSIVE DRINKING

Stephanie [M] began drinking at a young age. That first drink her friend's stepdad gave her hooked her. Wanting more, she agreed to have sex with him in exchange for alcohol. She invited the darkness in, and it kept her in its grip throughout her teenage years. In her early twenties, Stephanie gave her life to Christ and experienced the light of Jesus. It was the fresh start she needed.

A job at her church ended when the pastor declared living with her boyfriend invited a spirit of lust into the church. Anger at God welled up inside of her. "I felt put out, and I backslid. I went all out. I drank and smoked cigarettes and pot. Because I felt God took away my job and my church family, I wanted to pay Him back."

To numb her pain and anger, she once again invited the darkness of excessive drinking in. Her downward spiral lasted for eleven years. Stephanie drank every single day. "After every night of heavy drinking, I would look at my car to see if there was any damage to it. I knew I could have easily caused vehicular homicide while I was drunk. My addiction was that serious." She turned away from the light of God because she liked drinking. "I liked the smell and the taste. And how it made me feel. But I didn't like how it controlled me." After eleven years, Stephanie encountered a crossroads: would she continue allowing the alcohol to control her? Or would she fight to overcome her addiction?

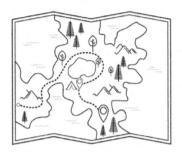

She chose to fight to overcome her addiction. Studying and memorizing Scriptures about being sober were weapons against the enemy who wanted her to stay in darkness. "I asked God to help me. I chose to feed my mind God's Word. And that had a huge impact. One day I realized I wasn't drinking anymore. Whatever you feed your mind is what conquers. In the end, God's Word conquered my desire to drink." At age forty, alcohol no longer controlled Stephanie. She was living clean and sober.

Eight years later, Stephanie continues to make the daily decision to seek God's light, avoiding any temptation to choose darkness. She is pursuing certification to become an alcohol and drug counselor. God is using what the enemy meant for Stephanie's harm to save others. He gave her a passion to help them to fight to overcome their addictions.

SONS OF LIGHT, DAUGHTERS OF DAY

How powerfully the words of 1 Thessalonians 5:4-8 apply to Stephanie's decision to shine the light of Jesus into the darkness she was inviting in. It says, "But friends, you're not in the dark, so how could you be taken off guard by any of this? You're sons of Light, daughters of Day. We live under wide open skies and know where we stand. So, let's not sleepwalk through life like those others. Let's keep our eyes open and be smart. People sleep at night and get drunk at night. But not us! Since we're creatures of Day, let's act like it. Walk out into the daylight sober, dressed up in faith, love, and the hope of salvation" (MSG).

Describe what it means for you to be a daughter of Day.

I encourage you to actively seek His light when you're dragged into darkness, or when you experience darkness that threatens to suffocate, or when illness throws you into darkness, and especially if you have invited darkness in. The *only* way to dispel any kind of darkness is to shine God's light. As a daughter of Day, you possess that light! Turn on your flashlight, dear friend.

In Ephesians 5:8-16, the apostle Paul contrasts living in darkness with the beauty of living in the light. Let's interact with these verses, so we will be well equipped to use our flashlights when darkness invades our path.

Underline the eight words or phrases Paul points out about choosing to live in darkness.

> "You groped your way through that murk once, but no longer. You're out in the open now. The bright light of Christ makes your way plain. So, no more stumbling around. Get on with it! The good, the right, the true—these are the actions appropriate for daylight hours. Figure out what will please Christ, and then do it. Don't waste your time on useless work, mere busywork, the barren pursuits of darkness. Expose

these things for the sham they are. It's a scandal when people waste their lives on things they must do in the darkness where no one will see. Rip those covers off the frauds and see how attractive they look in the light of Christ. Wake up from your sleep, climb out of your coffins; Christ will show you the light" (MSG).

These verses are clear about how we can choose to pursue darkness. Did you catch the eight words or phrases? If you didn't, go back and underline: *groped your way through that murk, stumbling around, barren pursuits of darkness, sham, scandal, where no one will see, frauds, and coffins.* If these words and phrases describe you, don't linger there! Instead, run from that trap of death and destruction. The only means of overcoming darkness is shining God's light. There is beauty, freedom, and life when we live in the light!

Please revisit those verses and highlight the five phrases about the beauty of living in the light.

Aren't they beautiful? If you didn't find all of them, they are *out in the open; the bright light of Christ makes your way plain; actions appropriate for daylight hours; how attractive they look in the light of Christ;* and *Christ will show you the light.*

YOU SHINE

God is the author and giver of light. He knew you would need His light when darkness enters your life as you are powerless to fight it on your own. God's light will shine hope into the dark crevices in your life. Satan's lies will have no room to take hold as His light fills you. You will no longer falsely believe the darkness will last forever. Strength to turn away from the darkness will course through your veins.

When God's light is in you, *you shine.* Yes ... you shine. You shine God's love and strength and healing and redemption, and so much more. People noticed when God's light overpowered the darkness in your life. Unbelievers especially wondered about the changes they saw in you. Perhaps, your transformation made them curious enough to ask questions. And so, you must "always be prepared to give an answer to everyone who asks you to give the reason for the hope that you have" (1 Peter 3:15). Imagine how your story gives them the tiniest shred of hope that the darkness clouding their life could be dispelled by the light you have. Are you ready to share that light?

Your story gives voice to the power of God's light. You shine brightly when you share your story. Thinking through the details of how the darkness in your life was overpowered by God's light will prepare you for a conversation should someone ask you about the changes they see in you.

Jot down a few phrases about the darkness you've experienced. Then write a few phrases about how God's light brought health, freedom, or restoration to your life.

MIGHTY WARRIOR IN GOD'S KINGDOM

Your journey has been tough and exhausting, but each piece of gear you've added to your backpack makes Satan tremble. He wasn't prepared for you to run to God's tent, or for you to study God's map to guide your journey. Communicating with God through prayer tunes your ear to God's voice instead of his. The enemy must shield his eyes when he sees God's light shining brightly in you. As powerful as Satan may believe he is, the gear you are using renders him weak and powerless. You are a mighty warrior in God's kingdom. Keep fighting to overcome!

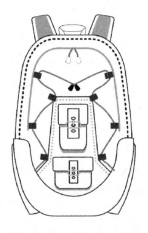

No doubt discussing the darkness you'll experience in this life has been a heavy load. However, carrying the light of Jesus in you makes your burdens light. We have more gear to add to our backpack, so shine your flashlight on our path as we walk toward the next mile marker.

Most often, it's in life's darkness that God prepares us for His best. 3
—Dr. Tony Evans, pastor and author

Who or What Is Magnified When You See Your Struggles?

> Worship is an act of war against the enemy of our hearts.1
> —Holley Gerth, author and podcaster

When life has shoved you in the dirt like the playground bully, you feel hurt, bruised, and perhaps even embarrassed. Maybe you're angry or frustrated. The enemy of your heart is suppressing your desire to express love, adoration, trust, and faith in God. Nothing makes him happier than seeing you shake your fist at God. He loves hearing you chide God for not answering your prayers. The incessant droning in your mind about how hard your struggle is, how weary you are, and how there isn't a way through fills the enemy with joy. He keeps hitting the replay button, hoping you'll believe his lies and give up. Don't do it.

Turn the tables on the enemy instead. Attack him by worshiping and praising God *while* you are struggling. Profess your trust in God's timing. Thank God for faithfully walking by your side. Express gratitude for His lovingkindness. Praise Him for supplying every one of your needs. Praise and thanksgiving combat the enemy's attacks most powerfully *while* you are suffering the deepest pain, *during* the long and lonely hours of desperation, and *when* it seems you will never rise above the relentless waves.

No one will need to remind you to worship and praise Him *after* your struggles are behind you. You won't be able to contain it. "Yes, God! Thank you, God!" will tumble out of your mouth. Just don't wait until you see a miracle or provision or healing to praise, worship, give thanks, and express gratitude to God. He's worthy of it every single day.

RAISE YOUR HANDS IN PRAISE

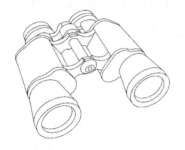

During the toughest times of your journey, pick up a pair of binoculars and put them to your eyes. What you see changes. Binoculars magnify, widening your perspective and allowing you to clearly see what is beyond your struggles. Often, when you are struggling, your focus is drawn to your pain, failure, betrayal, and suffering, or what is ten feet in front of you. Seeing beyond your struggle seems impossible.

A pair of binoculars will be our visual image for this part of our journey. With them, we are intentionally choosing to magnify God instead of our struggles. Offering thanksgiving even before we see healing or restoration might be challenging, but you'll quickly see how powerful it can be!

When God becomes your focus, you begin to see your struggle from His point of view. Psalm 145:17-19 explains His view: "Everything God does is right—the trademark on all his works is love. God's there, listening for all who pray, for all who pray and mean it. *He does what's best for those who fear him*—hears them call out and saves them" (MSG, emphasis mine). God providing what is best for you is a trustworthy promise.

Instead of shaking your fist at God, you'll raise your hands in praise. Realizing He answered your prayers in ways that are far better than you ever dreamed will cause you to shout thanksgivings. When you focus on Him, you are reminded that God will never turn His back on you. In fact, you marvel at how close He keeps you. He says, "Indeed, I have inscribed [a picture of] you on the palms of My hands ..." (Isaiah 49:16, AMPC). He sees you. He knows your name. He loves you with an unfailing love. He is acutely aware of the struggle you are facing, and even though you don't see how it will work out, you can trust He will *always* do what is best for you.

OUR EYES ARE ON YOU

The story of King Jehoshaphat of Judah is one of my favorites. Judah's enemies prepared to attack. Some of Jehoshaphat's men warned him: "A vast army is coming against you" (2 Chronicles 20: 2). Instead of puffing up with pride and foolishly believing the defeat of his enemies would be a piece of cake, King Jehoshaphat pulled out his multi-purpose tool and inquired of the LORD (verse 3).

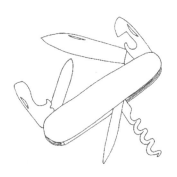

The king of Judah privately inquired of the LORD, and he publicly led the people in prayer (verses 6–12). Verse 12 is his counterattack. He lifted his eyes and declared he trusted God *during* that uncertain time. It says, "For we have no power to face this vast army that is attacking us. We do not know what to do, but our eyes are on you."

Reread and highlight the last sentence of his prayer.

King Jehoshaphat knew the best solution for not knowing what to do was to keep his eyes on God, not on the vast armies who were approaching. And not on the possibilities of defeat. He grabbed his binoculars, which magnified God instead of the approaching armies. After King Jehoshaphat's bold prayer, the prophet Jahaziel shared these words from the LORD: "Do not be afraid or discouraged because of this vast army. For the battle is not yours, but God's ... You will not have to fight this battle. Take up your positions; stand firm and see the deliverance the LORD will give you, Judah and Jerusalem. Do not be afraid; do not be discouraged. Go out to face them tomorrow, and the LORD will be with you" (verses 15, 17).

Underline the directives they were to follow instead of falling prey to their fears.

King Jehoshaphat, all the people, and the Levite priests responded boldly: "Jehoshaphat bowed down with his face to the ground and all the people fell down in worship before the LORD. Then some Levites stood up and praised the LORD, the God of Israel, with a very loud voice" (verses 18-19).

Highlight their responses. Now describe *when* they praised and worshipped God.

BEGAN TO SING AND PRAISE

In verse 21, King Jehoshaphat appointed men in his army to sing to the LORD and praise him with these words: "Give thanks to the LORD, for his love endures forever." Watch what happened next! "As they began to sing and praise, the LORD set ambushes against the men of

Ammon and Moab and Mount Seir who were invading Judah, and they were defeated" (verse 22).

Write this sentence below: Their worship and praise were weapons in God's hands.

Describe how those words impact you.

Jehoshaphat and the people didn't just praise and worship *before* and *during* their encounter with their enemies. They also did so *after* the victory: "They entered Jerusalem and went to the temple of the LORD with harps and lyres and trumpets" (verse 28).

REVEAL HER PURPOSE IN LIFE

After months of suffering high fevers, stomach aches, and fatigue, an infectious disease doctor ran tests on six-year-old Chloe[N]. The tests revealed Crohn's disease was attacking her from her mouth to her rectum. Reducing the inflammation required immunosuppressive treatment every seven weeks. Her treatment regimen worked well for four years. Then, a CT scan and colonoscopy to determine why the medicine was no longer working showed her intestines were so swollen that nothing could pass through. A couple of weeks in and out of the hospital led to her needing a feeding tube to stabilize her. Chloe remembers, "It was scary, but I felt the peace of God. I learned to trust God. I knew in the blink of an eye; things could be different."

Years later at a summer church camp, Chloe asked God to reveal her purpose in life. "By the time I left camp, I knew my purpose was to share my love for God through singing." Singing with the worship team at church was frightening at first, but those listening knew Chloe's voice was a gift from God. Words of praise to God consistently swirled in her mind, so she began putting those words into song lyrics.

THAT'S WHY I SING

While spending time with her grandfather who was fighting cancer, Chloe wrote a song titled "That's Why I Sing." She sang the following words to her grandfather as encouragement to worship God even during his darkest days.

> *You're my umbrella when the rain is falling down on me*
> *You're my light when the darkness is surrounding me*
> *You're the healer when sickness is overwhelming me*
> *God, you are good*
> *You never leave*
> *You're always right next to me*

Cancer ended her grandfather's earthly life. During his last days, her words comforted him and encouraged him to put his focus on Jesus instead of his struggles. Those lyrics are a constant reminder to Chloe as she daily fights the pain and fatigue from her ongoing struggle with Crohn's disease. Chloe's wisdom shined through when she shared, "In my life, I've experienced many storms and struggles, but it is in those places where my dependency on God grows stronger. Praise and worship are gifts we have for when we don't know what to say. I will always sing and write songs of praise to the Father."

And she has done just that. Chloe continues to lead worship at her church. Currently, her focus is earning a degree in worship studies with minors in Christian counseling and children and family studies. She dreams of being a full-time worship leader.

TURN OUR FOCUS TO GOD

Chloe's song lyrics are powerful. We can relate, can't we? Think of a time when rain was *falling down* on you. Or a time when *darkness was surrounding* you. Or when *sickness was overwhelming* you. It is challenging to worship during those times because we naturally tend to focus on the rain or the darkness or the sickness that is ten feet in front

of us. Those struggles loom large, literally blocking our view. The enemy has us right where he wants us: unable to tear our eyes away from his magnification of our struggles. It's easy to fall into pity or anger or accept the lie that things will never change. Remember this: the enemy will continue to cloud our vision *as long as we allow him to.*

When you choose to put binoculars to your eyes, the enemy loses his power to cloud your vision. Your perspective changes, raising your eyes above your struggles. The lens magnifies God, not your struggles. Your struggles might not instantly disappear, but your view of them now includes a miracle-working, enemy-destroying God who promises to protect you from trouble and surround you with songs of deliverance (Psalm 32:7). Did you catch that? He's singing songs of deliverance over you. He is singing over you!

Pause for a moment and visualize God surrounding you with songs of deliverance. Describe how knowing this fills you with praise and worship.

HOW YOU WORSHIP

Maybe you're not comfortable singing praises to God. That's ok. You might be wondering if you could just skip the whole praise and worship piece of gear as you love God but aren't comfortable expressing it outwardly. The good news is it doesn't have to come from your vocal cords. How you worship and express praise are as unique as you are. Some, like Chloe, are gifted with voices that open the heavens. A brush in the hands of an artist expresses worship as color forms a picture on a canvas. A poet strings words of worship together that transport the reader to the heart of God.

When you serve others, your heart and actions magnify and glorify the one who is the greatest servant of all: Jesus. Taking a homemade meal to a widow and dispelling her loneliness with conversation worships God. Buying a pair of shoes for a homeless person honors God. Folding baskets upon baskets of laundry so your large family is ready for the week ahead worships God. Calling a friend who is struggling to check on her is music to God's ears. Pouring wisdom that you learned during your struggles into a young person extols God.

WORK BECOMES WORSHIP

Pastor Rick Warren described a way we worship God that you may not have considered. He believes, "Work becomes worship when you dedicate it to God and perform it with an awareness of His presence."[2] The mechanic who not only repairs a sputtering engine but also replaces the dry rotted windshield wipers worships God with his work, making it possible for a single mother to drive safely to her job. Hearing the words *not guilty* after you spent months defending an innocent woman praises God as He knows the sacrifices you made to prevent a miscarriage of justice. The countless lives saved when doctors and nurses worked in dangerous conditions during the Coronavirus pandemic was a beautiful expression of when work becomes worship.

No matter how 'behind the scenes' your job is or if your name is known around the world for the work you do, your work becomes worship when you dedicate it to God. Perhaps, you've never considered your work as worship. Let's explore how God equipped you to serve and love others through your work. Our world needs your work because it contributes to the betterment of our society. When you dedicate your work to God, it is a fragrant aroma of worship and praise.

Describe your work.

How has God equipped you to serve and love others through your work?

Take a moment now to pray and offer the work you do as a fragrant offering of worship and praise.

FELT AS IF GOD DIDN'T LOVE HER

Despite living with chronic health issues for decades, Erin º chose years ago to dedicate her work to God and perform it as praise and worship.

A little backstory first. Erin was diagnosed with lupus at age eighteen. Then, her nerve endings felt 'on fire' all day and night. She fought that pain, but eventually testing revealed fibromyalgia was the name for that pain. Two chronic illnesses should be enough for anyone to fight, but Erin's liver, kidneys, stomach, intestines, joints, and ribs stayed inflamed for several years, finally leading to a diagnosis of Crohn's disease at age twenty-five.

Her anger toward God grew with each additional diagnosis. It felt as if God didn't love her. It didn't seem as if He cared about her pain or struggles. Erin's doctors encouraged her to stop working and rest to allow her body time to heal. Reading Priscilla Shirer's book, *God Is Able*, caused Erin to rethink her anger toward God. She realized, "My pain subsided when I drew close to God. I began to see He truly did care for and love me. It felt as if He was holding me. I learned when life is tough, you have to choose to plant your feet and look to God no matter what. Praise Him for His presence. Praise Him for His mercy and grace. Praise Him for His unfailing love."

BROKEN BUT PRICELESS

As Erin's heart opened to God again, she began piecing together a book where she would explore what it meant to be broken but priceless. Erin realized in addition to a book, a website ministry could be a central location for those who fought chronic illnesses to share resources, encourage one another, and spur one another on to live their lives to the fullest. Founded in 2010, the 'Broken but Priceless' website set out to accomplish those goals. Her ministry's tagline is: "Even though our bodies may be broken, we are priceless in God's eyes."

Erin's work to support others with chronic illnesses became worship. While she has worked part-time off and on over the years, her primary focus has been serving the chronic illness community through the Broken but Priceless ministry. What started as a website with articles grew to speaking opportunities where she could encourage large groups of people who daily fight various chronic illnesses. More than a decade later, Erin's quarterly online magazine reaches readers around the world. Additionally, Erin works at a Christian home for children who experienced pain and trauma during their young lives. Sharing God's love with those children brings her great joy.

RENDER THE ENEMY POWERLESS

Praise and worship are spiritual weapons. Weapons that deflect the lies of the enemy and prevent his fiery darts from penetrating our hearts. These weapons make the enemy flee. Finding words of praise or singing songs of worship *during* the struggle is often difficult. The enemy is intentionally making it difficult. So, you must be more intentional and more persistent than he is.

As you continue to create your survival guide, be intentional about collecting verses that you can speak out loud *during* your struggle. Render the enemy powerless by persistently speaking those verses out loud in faith. As you do so, believe He is working, especially when you can't see it. Thanking God for meeting your needs even before you see His provision dumbfounds the enemy. Expressing gratitude for the strength you've gained while fighting your struggle steals his power.

As you read the following verses, underline, highlight, or make notes about the verses that bolster your faith and stir up your courage. Praise God as you proclaim these truths over your life.

"Today you are going into battle against your enemies. Do not be fainthearted or afraid; do not panic or be terrified by them. For the LORD your God is the one who goes with you to fight for you against your enemies to give you victory" (Deuteronomy 20:3-4).

"Be strong and courageous. Do not be afraid or terrified because of them, for the LORD your God goes with you; he will never leave you nor forsake you" (Deuteronomy 31:6).

"Let the beloved of the LORD rest secure in him, for he shields him all day long; and the one the LORD loves rests between his shoulders" (Deuteronomy 33:12).

"I have heard your prayer and seen your tears: I will heal you" (2 Kings 20:5).

"They were helped in fighting them, and God delivered the Hagrites and all their allies into their hands, because they cried out to him *during* the battle. He answered their prayers, because they trusted in him" (1 Chronicles 5:20, emphasis mine).

"But you, LORD, do not be far from me. You are my strength: come quickly to help me" (Psalm 22:19).

"The LORD is my strength and my shield; my heart trusts in him, and he helps me. My heart leaps for joy, and with my song I praise him" (Psalm 28:7).

"Let your face shine on your servant; save me in your unfailing love" (Psalm 31:16).

"Send me your light and your faithful care, let them lead me; let them bring me to your holy mountain, to the place where you dwell" (Psalm 43:3).

"Cast your cares on the LORD and he will sustain you; he will never let the righteous be shaken" (Psalm 55:22).

"You are my strength, I watch for you; you, God, are my fortress, my God on whom I can rely" (Psalm 59:9).

"You will keep in perfect peace those whose minds are steadfast, because they trust in you" (Isaiah 26:3).

"LORD, be gracious to us; we long for you. Be our strength every morning, our salvation in time of distress" (Isaiah 33:2).

"I will turn their mourning into gladness; I will give them comfort and joy instead of sorrow" (Jeremiah 31:13).

"Truly I tell you, if you have faith as small as a mustard seed, you can say to this mountain, 'Move from here to there.' And it will move. Nothing will be impossible for you" (Matthew 17:10).

"Come with me by yourselves to a quiet place and get some rest" (Mark 6:31).

"I have given you authority to trample on snakes and scorpions and to overcome all the power of the enemy; nothing will harm you" (Luke 10:19).

"Being confident of this, that he who began a good work in you will carry it on to completion until the day of Christ Jesus" (Philippians 1:6).

"Let us then approach God's throne of grace with confidence, so that we may receive mercy and find grace to help us in our time of need" (Hebrews 4:16).

"Let us throw off everything that hinders and the sin that so easily entangles. And let us run with perseverance the race marked out for us, fixing our eyes on Jesus" (Hebrews 12:1-2).

In no way is this an exhaustive list of verses to speak out loud during your struggle. Please use the space below to add verses you already speak aloud when you praise and worship God.

FOCUS ON GOD

Now that you've gained experience with using binoculars to fix your eyes on God, I imagine you feel less stressed, less anxious, more confident, and more hopeful. You will gain these feelings and more when you take your eyes off the struggle ten feet in front of you and focus on God instead. What an awesome piece of gear these binoculars are proving to be! May I encourage you to add a colorful sticky note to the edge of these pages for easy reference in the future?

There's one more piece of gear to add to your backpack in the mile ahead. Remember, you aren't just collecting things; you are learning about or reminding yourself of the powerful tools you have access to that equip you to courageously fight to overcome the struggles in your path. While we journey on, will you join me in a song of praise?

> Satan so hates the genuine praise of Christ that his fiery darts of discouragement are not effective against us when we respond in praise.3
> —Author William Thrasher

mile 08

How Will You Remember Your Journey?

> Pay attention to the chapters of the story I'm giving you.1
> —Shelly Miller, author

In a video session for her Bible study *Entrusted*, Beth Moore admitted, "I am happiest when I'm learning. I love to study."² Her description could easily be said of me. Anytime I read a nonfiction book, I do not just read it. I read it to learn something new. You'll find underlined sentences and phrases which convicted me. Notes litter the margin with my reflections about what I'm learning. Brightly colored sticky notes define unfamiliar words.

You may not relate to Beth Moore's proclamation of being happiest when she's learning like I do, but I hope you're underlining sentences and making notes in the margins of this book. Remember, you've been creating a survival guide to help you fight to overcome your current struggle. And it will be ready and easily accessible when a future unexpected turn threatens to knock you off your path.

I read Shelly Miller's book, *Rhythms of Rest*, during a month-long leave of absence to address my unrelenting fatigue. Her words about the importance of rest didn't just speak to me. They yelled at me. I littered the margins with notes, and I double underlined her words in the opening quote of this mile.

Read it aloud: "Pay attention to the chapters of the story I'm giving you."

Those words convicted me. My weariness and frustration from unrelenting fatigue dulled my attentiveness. I wasn't paying attention. Let me say that again: I wasn't paying attention. Chapters of my story were unfolding, but I was completely inattentive and unaware. I was so focused on the effort it took to make it through a day that I missed gifts scattered along my path. The fatigue *and* the gifts were the chapters of my story. I was focusing on what was ten feet in front me—the fatigue—instead of seeing the gifts all around me.

I knew recording the struggles *and* the gifts would help me pay better attention. Journaling gave me the space to record my journey—a travel log of sorts. If you don't have a travel log packed, you'll need one. Not only will it give you space to process the struggles you're facing, but a travel log will also help you pay attention to the lessons you're learning, the gifts along your path, and a permanent location  to record just how far you've come on your journey of overcoming. The visual image of a notebook and pen will represent your travel log.

As you read and interact along this mile, look for the eight benefits of using a travel log. Highlight each of the benefits with one color. I'll ask you to share those at the end of this mile.

ONE THOUSAND GIFTS

Ann Voskamp's book, *One Thousand Gifts: A Dare to Live Fully Right Where You Are,* is the second most read book in my library. Multiple colors of ink underline incredibly insightful passages. Notes fill the margins about how I need to record my blessings. Ann's travel log can be found in her books and on her website, annvoskamp.com. She process her journey in words, as well as capturing it with her camera.

In her book, Ann explained her journey of coming to understand the power of gratitude *during* her days of struggle, as well as the days of her ordinary life. She studied God's Word and learned the meaning of eucharisteo: *grace, thanksgiving, joy.* As she contemplated the meaning of the word, she asked herself: "How in the world, for the sake of my joy, do I learn to use eucharisteo to overcome my one ugly and self-destructive habit of ingratitude (that habit that causes both my cosmic and daily fall) with the saving habit of gratitude—that would lead me back to deep God-communion?"[3]

Ann practices *eucharisteo* to overcome her ugly and self-destructive habit of ingratitude. Do you have an ugly and self-destructive habit of ingratitude, too? If so, describe how you've been ungrateful.

Eucharisteo means grace, thanksgiving, and joy. Have you focused so much on your struggle that you've missed opportunities to see grace and joy in your life?

If you've seen moments of grace and joy, have you thanked God?

GRATEFUL FOR ALL THE GIFTS

Maybe you've realized you have been ungrateful for the grace and joy interspersed among your struggles. You know you need to be grateful for the good days that fall in between your days of struggle, but you just don't know how. Ann wasn't sure either, so she took on a dare to name one thousand blessings—one thousand gifts—over the course of a year. Throughout her book, Ann chronicled her life as she chose to be grateful for *all* the gifts. The gifts that filled her with happiness, and the gifts that were tough. Yes, you read that correctly. *All* the gifts, including the tough ones.

How can the tough struggles you've been through be gifts? Maybe you're not ready to make that declaration. Maybe your pain is still brutally raw. Its venom is poisoning your mind and body. Then it must come out. Record it on the pages of your travel log. Write your hurt in big bold red letters and then scribble over it in the darkest black marker you can find. Fill up as many pages as you need with adjectives or phrases describing how your struggle is impacting your life. Remember the Dear Struggle letter from mile 02? If words won't come, be assured tears speak when your words cannot.

In my journal during my leave of absence, I recorded my frustrations: what I believed I was missing by having to sleep so much; how a dense fog clouded my mind every single day; and how irritable it made me feel. When I wrote the word *fatigue*, a rush of emotions threatened to swallow me. That word defined me. And I hated that it did. Yes, my body physically needed to rest, but that wasn't the only struggle I faced. I felt pain, but it wasn't physical pain. My pain was emotional and mental, which felt worse as only I could feel how much I was suffering. I felt like a prisoner in my body and my mind—with no hope of release.

Before I could declare any of it was a gift, it was imperative I call out the pain and hurt. I couldn't blame anyone, including God. No 'why me' questions. I had to extricate my thoughts and emotions about my tough struggle, ridding my mind of their poison. Until I saw it on the page, there was no way I could begin to think of any of it as a gift. Slowly, I did. And you will, too.

Let's practice. Write a few phrases describing your pain.

What is one thing that you could consider to be a gift during this painful time?

In the Afterword of *One Thousand Gifts*, Ann wrote, "Blessings keep our awareness of life's holy potential ever present."[4] Meditate on her words and then write your response below.

A LEGACY FOR MY BOYS

Recording your daily gifts changes your perspective. You'll slowly slip out of focusing on your troubles and slip into focusing on all the good in your life. When I interviewed Cori [P], I heard her say the words *mass, colorectal cancer, colostomy,* and *surgery* several times. However, they were grossly overshadowed by the number of times I heard her say the words *grateful* and *full of gratitude*. I asked if she'd read Ann Voskamp's book. She replied, "No, I haven't, but it sounds like my gratitude journal." I had to know more, so I asked her to elaborate.

Cori's travel log is a gratitude journal. By the time she heard the word *cancer-free,* she'd filled three gratitude journals. Instead of focusing on her struggle, pain, and fears, she laser-focused on and recorded the daily gifts that were covering her path. She started her travel log the day she heard the word *mass* and has written in it every day since then. "When I'm having a tough day, I go back and  reflect on all the things I have to be grateful for. I want my journals to be a legacy for my boys."

Here's an excerpt from her journal: Today I woke up feeling scared, but I immediately knew I needed to change my mindset. God is in the boat with me through this storm. I am grateful for this day. I am grateful for a loving and hard-working husband. I am blessed to be able to exude joy, life, and energy to others. I am grateful for sunshine and my patio. I am grateful for the power of prayer.

Another excerpt: I'm grateful for joy—the inward joy that comes from knowing and trusting God. Inward joy defeats discouragement. I'm grateful I'm protected by the armor of God. I will have that today when the doctor calls with my biopsy results.

An excerpt after her surgery: I'm grateful for memories of sweet Grams. Grateful to have had her as a role model of strength and grace and the times I feel her with me. Grateful the tumor is gone. Grateful for Dr. Delaney and his skilled hands. Grateful for the ultimate Physician.

Could Cori have made it through her cancer struggle without her gratitude journal? Maybe. I contend her journal filled her with so much strength, peace, joy, trust, and faith, her body had no choice but to cooperate with man-made treatments and God's healing hand.

In February of 2022, Cori celebrated her five-year cancer-free anniversary. Sometimes the thought of recurrence sneaks in, but she reminds herself not to worry as God has already taken care of her healing. She's grateful her good health allows her to work full-time with her husband, Eddie. Travel, hiking, sunsets, friends, and family will most assuredly be part of her future when she and Eddie retire.

MAKING GRATITUDE A PART OF YOUR JOURNEY

By recording Scriptures and everything she is grateful for in her journal, Cori has written those affirmations on her heart as it says in Proverbs 1:1-3 (AMPC): "My son, do not forget my teaching, but let your heart keep my commandments; For length of days and years of life [worth living] and tranquility and prosperity [the wholeness of life's blessings] they will add to you. Do not let mercy and kindness and truth leave you [instead let these qualities define you]; Bind them [securely] around your neck, write them on the tablet of your heart."

When we are struggling, it's easy to lose our focus. Sometimes we dissect our challenge and examine every side, hoping we can change it or predict the outcome. Neither of which we can control. We desperately try to answer the 'what if' questions as if those hypothetical answers could give us hope. Instead of hope, those answers often sow seeds of discouragement and anger.

Gratitude, on the other hand, takes the focus off the situation, the outcomes, and the need to control it. It fixes our eyes on God, inviting us to see the small and large blessings all around us. Maybe you've found it hard to see those blessings. When you record those blessings in your travel log, you are paying attention to your story!

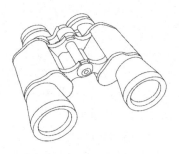

Theologian Thomas Merton spent his years as a monk contemplating—viewing or considering with attention—the world around him and choosing to be filled with a deep gratitude for life. He wrote, "Contemplation is the highest expression of man's intellectual and spiritual life. It is that life itself, fully awake, fully active, fully aware that it is alive. It is spiritual wonder. It is spontaneous awe at the sacredness of life, of being. It is gratitude for life, for awareness and for being. It is a vivid realization of the fact that life and being in us proceed from an invisible, transcendent and infinitely abundant Source."[5]

Reread Thomas Merton's quote. This time read it out loud. Do you agree with him? Describe why you agree or disagree.

REMEMBER ALL YOU LEARNED

Suppose you had the opportunity to step away from the craziness of your daily life and take several classes that focused on your passion.

Describe your passion.

Now, back to the opportunity before you. After taking these classes, you could easily be ready to change the course of your career or even your life. You will be equipped with knowledge beyond what Google could provide. Exploring your passion and fine-tuning what you are to do with that passion will almost draw a complete map of your future steps. A network of like-minded individuals who will support you and hold you accountable will join you on your journey. By encouraging you to conquer your fears, these classes will strengthen you.

Oh, wait. There is one caveat. You can't take any notes. None. Nada. You'll just have to rely on your memory. "Wait. I can't remember all that information!" you say. "What if I need to refer back to that information when I encounter unexpected turns on my new adventure?" Sorry. You'll have to rely on your memory. You took the classes. Just remember what you learned!

Pause for a minute and think about how not taking notes when studying your passion would prevent you from getting the most out of that opportunity. Jot down a few of your thoughts.

There is much to be learned from the time you feel yourself being pulled off course until you ease back onto your path. You'll want to remember what you learned. Of course, the best method for remembering what you're learning is to take good notes. Research shows you have a much higher chance of remembering the lessons you're learning if you take notes. Detailed, dissertation-like notes are not required. Just jotting down the knowledge and wisdom you're gaining. Notes to process the fine-tuning happening in your life. Add in the notes of encouragement from those who are walking beside you. Instead of fussing at you, your Kindergarten teacher would encourage you to doodle or draw pictures or scribble words about how you're facing your fears and living to talk about it. Just imagine the legacy you'll be leaving!

I AM A MIRACLE

Jessica [Q] remembers many details about the day she and her boyfriend, Nate, were hit head-on by a truck. The motorcycle they were riding was a tangled mess. She was thrown eighty feet into a ditch. Nate suffered many injuries and a heart attack before passing away at the hospital. Jessica sustained serious injuries. Her parents were told she had a 50/50 chance of surviving. Seven surgeries put Jessica back together. She was bed bound for almost a year before learning to walk again.

Jessica's Facebook page blew up with news about the accident. Hundreds of friends and family posted prayers and well wishes. Jessica's mom began posting updates about her progress. A travel log of Jessica's journey was forming. Jessica began adding to the travel log.

July 7, 2012 (14 days post-accident): I count my blessings every day I am alive and know I am a miracle.

July 16, 2012 (25 days post-accident): There is nowhere to go but up. I'm gonna fight. I've been journaling to see how far I've come since the day of the accident.

August 9, 2012 (47 days post-accident): If we have ever wondered about the limits of our strength and our ability to endure, our experience of loss will tell us so much. Our life is shaken to the foundation, but we survive. We are in the hands of the One who can. Unless I bind it to me, hopelessness doesn't last forever.

Please read the next entry carefully. Underline the words Jessica used as she worked through her challenges. Then, highlight when she expressed gratitude.

> **August 25, 2012 (60 days post-accident):** I'm trying to confront my adversity and the inevitable questions evoked by my suffering. Answers are sought, and encouragement is needed. I simply feel isolated right now, like no one has experienced this much pain at one time. Taking away so much of my life in one swipe. I'm reminded of Job. Growth comes, then struggle, and vice versa. Each season has its purpose. The pressures we face test us, and our faith can show us and others our true colors. I should not try to get out of these seasons prematurely. I should let it do its work, so I can become mature and well-developed. I struggle during this waiting period wanting to hurry, maybe attempting to make permanent decisions on temporary circumstances. Reminder to self: every situation doesn't call for immediate action. Patience comes from trust in a future I cannot see. My suffering may be part of a bigger plan, something beyond the realm of comprehension. For now, I sit and wait. Strengthening my mind, body, and soul to prepare for what tomorrow brings.

THE WRITTEN RECORD

You just witnessed Jessica struggling hard and caught a glimpse of the wisdom she was gaining. Every word she wrote as she fought to overcome held extreme value. Did you see the dichotomy of how she processed all the pain she'd been through and then in the next line, she thanked God for the numerous gifts she saw all around her?

When I interviewed Jessica, she referenced her travel log often as it was the written record of the specific details of her struggle. Every high and every low of her recovery was recorded there. Each literal step she took after the accident was a success that needed to be documented. Because her travel log is an important part of her journey, she read aloud certain passages to me. Jessica teared up at times as she relived the hurt, the loneliness, and the pain she felt during her recovery. She glowed when she described how her family and friends showered her in love, naming each person as a gift. In between the struggle and pain, she saw God. She was attentive to the chapters of her story.

God was her constant companion throughout her journey. Her heart was receptive to what He was teaching. She recorded it as she didn't want to forget the lessons she was learning, the wisdom she was gaining, and the testimony of God's love she was seeing. Jessica's travel log is her legacy of God fighting with her to overcome her physical injuries and her broken heart, as well as how the accident impacted every facet of her life. Several years after the accident, Jessica was given a second chance when she married an honest, hard-working, Christ-centered man named Nick.

Jessica and Nick live in the country on a small homestead where she raises pets and rehabilitates wildlife. She continues to work in the veterinary field, but now as a manager instead of a vet tech due to her limited mobility. The stars on a clear night remind her how small she is. In contrast, she loves the large role God has given her to share her miraculous story. She dreams of having a less painful body, but her scars remind her of how far she has come. Jessica hopes to continue to inspire one person at a time to never give up.

BENEFITS OF A TRAVEL LOG

Ann Voskamp's dare to record one thousand gifts, Cori's gratitude journal, and Jessica's Facebook posts are three examples of travel logs. Your travel log doesn't have to look like theirs. Yours needs to be uniquely you. The possibilities are endless.

Go back through this mile of our journey and find the eight benefits of having a travel log you highlighted. Jot them down below.

1.
2.
3.
4.
5.
6.
7.
8.

In case you missed one or more of the benefits, they are: *You will pay better attention to your life. You will begin to change your perspective. A place to record your frustrations/how your struggle is impacting your life. A place to record the gifts all around you/your gratitude. A place to record what you are learning about yourself/others/life. A place to record how your attitude/strength/relationship with God is being fine-tuned. A place to record your progress and reflect on how far you've come. A place to record encouragement and support from family, friends, and strangers.*

If you already keep a travel log, you might have been able to spot the benefits easily as you already see those benefits in your life. Which one connects with you most? Explain why.

If you haven't been using a travel log, did one of the benefits persuade you to start a travel log? Which one?

Not all these benefits will matter to you. Instead, focus on the ones that do. I hope seeing these benefits in action will encourage you to start a travel log. I promise you won't regret it. Your future self, when she rereads all the entries, will marvel at what a stronger, wiser, more resilient overcomer you are. She will thank you.

YOUR FIGHT VERSE

Go back through this book, reviewing each of the times you highlighted a verse or put a star by a verse that could become your fight verse. Pick 'the one' that resonates with you, filling you with courage, boldness, and determination to fight to overcome whatever struggle *dares* to cross your path.

Write your fight verse below.

I encourage you to memorize it, so it will come to mind when you need it most.

> I can shake off everything as I write; my sorrows disappear, my courage is reborn.6
> —Anne Frank, young author who perished in the Holocaust

REST & RECHARGE

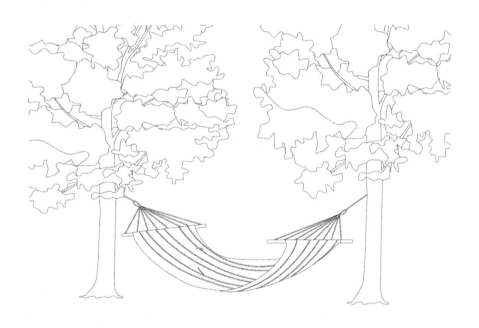

Rest and motion, unrelieved and unchecked, are equally destructive.1
—Benjamin Cardoza, attorney

Since that first trail sign that marked your unexpected turn, we've traveled eight miles together. You've completed half of the journey! That unexpected turn could have defeated you or tempted you to give up, but you refused to allow that challenge to stop you. Instead, you committed to creating a survival guide to help you navigate that unfamiliar territory. You wanted to learn every lesson the struggles were meant to teach you, so you engaged with the content and actively participated by highlighting important passages and answering the questions. Great job, friend!

Every step of those eight miles encouraged you to trust in and rely on the master navigator: God. You need Him because Jesus promised difficulties will continue to intersect your path: "I've told you all this so that trusting me, you will be unshakable and assured, deeply at peace. In this godless world you will continue to experience difficulties. But take heart! I've conquered the world," (John 16:33, MSG).

But take heart! His sacrifice on the cross defeated any power sin or death could ever hold over you. His resurrection fully demonstrated sin and death would be limited to your earthly life. Overcoming sin and death by offering forgiveness and the hope of eternal life destroyed the enemy's plan of keeping you separated from God. Because He overcame, you can too. Thank you, Jesus!

TRAINS HIS SOLDIERS

The April 10 devotion in *Streams in the Desert* connects so closely with the topic of this book that I would be remiss not to share it with you. It says, "God trains His soldiers not in tents of ease and luxury but by causing them to endure lengthy marches and difficult service. He makes them wade across streams, swim through rivers, climb mountains, and walk many tiring miles with heavy backpacks."[2] Can you relate?

Have ease and luxury been part of your struggle? Not even close. Lengthy marches and difficult service? Yes! Wade across murky streams? Too many to count. Swim through rivers with swift rapids? Most definitely. Climb steep mountains. Ugghhh ... yes. Walk many tiring miles with heavy backpacks? Absolutely! But, as heavy as your backpack is, you know the value of its contents. You wouldn't journey a mile without your backpack and every piece of gear in it, would you?

These pieces of gear aren't just essential in your fight to overcome life's tough challenges. They are integral to your everyday life. Your uneventful, routine life. Those days, weeks, or years unencumbered by struggle, trouble, strife, or obstacles. You want God involved in every day of your life, so you're incorporating these pieces of gear into your daily life.

You've discovered your daily connection with God sustains you. When you incorporate the gear into your daily life, you feel nourished. God fills you with joy. He fuels your passion. He showers you with His unfailing love and kindness. He breathes abundant life in you. He strengthens you. You are ready to face any struggle, obstacle, challenge, or trouble.

HOW THE GEAR EMPOWERS YOU TO FIGHT TO OVERCOME

You're returning home after the first half of your journey, so it's time to unpack and assess. Open your backpack and spread out the pieces of gear.

Look at each of the visual symbols. Can you easily identify what each represents?

Beside each piece of gear, write what it represents and how it empowers you to fight to overcome. If you need to, review your notes.

Rope represents

Tent represents

Map represents

Multi-purpose tool represents

CHALLENGES WON'T STOP ME | 143

Flashlight represents

Binoculars represents

Travel log represents

Grab a different colored pen. Beside each piece of gear, describe how you experienced God when you implemented it in your fight to overcome.

The miles ahead will test your commitment to overcoming life's tough challenges. Your desire to thrive will be challenged. What's the best way to prepare for the second half of your journey? Intentionally and consistently use your gear. Knowing your gear—inside and out—is the best preparation. Take apart each piece of gear and examine its purpose. Test your gear's reliability and trustworthiness. Determine if consistent use exhausts each piece of gear or strengthens it. Assess your mental and emotional fortitude after a few days of not using your gear. Yes, I'm encouraging you to go a few days without your gear. Awareness of how you feel without it will be far more convincing than anything I could say. I look forward to seeing your well-loved and well-worn gear when we meet again.

REST AND RECHARGE

We've only traveled half our journey. You will need plenty of energy to finish strong. I encourage you to rest and recharge. Your body, brain, and emotions need rest because fighting to overcome takes an incredible amount of energy, focus, and mental fortitude. Not to mention how the stress of it is impacting you. Aches and pain attack your body during the day while you're trying to work and at night while you're trying to sleep. Your brain is working overtime, trying to process every detail of your struggle, as well as how to protect itself from potential danger. Your emotions have been stomped on, jerked this way and that, and left out in the pounding rain.

Self-care is a must. Not the kind culture tells you to take. This self-care isn't focusing on you and your needs to the exclusion of others. Neglecting others isn't who you are. Instead, your self-care includes resting your body, brain, and emotions. Intentional rest recharges you, allowing you to regain the energy and strength you've depleted. Intentional rest inspires and invigorates you. Dr. Saundra Dalton-Smith says it best: "Like you, my life is not all rainbows and sunshine. Some days are easier than others. But every day I make a choice to rest, and it has transformed me. Rest has become my go-to source for strength, creativity, productivity, peace, joy, hope, and contentment. I've found it to be the best-kept secret in medicine."[3]

Experience the benefits of rest by taking a nap, spending time in nature, or soaking up the sun. Recharge by enjoying activities which take your mind off your struggles. Play with your kids, soaking in their joy. Schedule a dinner out and connect with friends. Turn your phone off. Laugh until you can't speak. Stretch your body. Invite a friend to 'puzzle' with you. Take a silent retreat and connect with God. Paint a picture or spin some clay. Whatever you choose to do, take the time to really experience it. And enjoy it!

YOU ARE AN OVERCOMER

As we part ways for a bit, I want you to know it's been an honor to journey with you. When I think of the grit, determination, resilience, and perseverance you've shown thus far, it is clear you are an overcomer.

How do I know? Simple. You wouldn't have made it this far if you weren't a fighter. Much was required of you these first eight miles, and you made it! Please rest and recharge. Before long, it will be time for us to meet at mile marker 09. Be ready, and bring your backpack filled with your gear. We will keep moving forward. I look forward to seeing you there!

"But those who wait for the Lord [who expect, look for, and hope in Him] shall change and renew their strength and power; they shall lift their wings and mount up [close to God] as eagles [mount up to the sun]; they shall run and not be weary, they shall walk and not faint *or* become tired."

Isaiah 40:31 (AMPC)

ACKNOWLEDGEMENTS

It definitely takes a village to raise a child, but it also takes a village to birth a book. I am grateful for the people in my village who believed in me and the message of this book.

Thank you to ...

My overcomer family. Each of you in this ever-growing family of courageous women is precious to me. Thank you for trusting me with your stories of overcoming. Your continued friendship, encouragement, and love fuels my passion for sharing the message of fighting to overcome.

My beta readers, Carmela, Heather, Shannon, and Tami. You honored me by not offering lofty praises about my book. Instead, your constructive feedback was invaluable. Thank you for helping to make this book an even better resource for those who are fighting to overcome life's tough challenges.

My advocate, Julie Wood. Thank you for your legal expertise and helping me understand how to protect my overcomers and their stories, as well as my work.

My editor, Marcie Bridges. Grateful we met and ate breakfast together all those years ago at Blue Ridge Mountain Christian Writers Conference. Thank you for catching my mistakes and suggesting even better ways to express my thoughts.

My proofreader, NaKeya Bazemore. Thank you for proofreading the last, and the last, and I promise the last version. Your eagle eye caught my errors and those that autocorrect made.

My interior designer, Catherine Posey. Thank you for creating an amazing interior design for my words.

My book cover designer, Hannah Linder. Thank you for creating a cover that beautifully represents the journey of overcoming and thriving.

My parents, Frank and Glenda Cole. Thank you for instilling an overcomer attitude in me way before I could have chosen it for myself. Because you decided my stroke would not define me or limit me, I developed resilience and perseverance. Not matter what challenge dares to intersect my path, I'm never giving up!

My God. I am humbled and grateful that You entrusted me with the message of overcoming and thriving. Thank you for every open door and opportunity you've granted me. May this book bring You glory.

APPENDIX OF OVERCOMER STORIES

This appendix contains the location of each overcomer's story on my website, which may be accessed at melonybrown.com. Each overcomer listed below gave written permission to use a snippet of her story in this book.

A. Melony's story, "God's Got This," 21 July 2016, Stories tab.
B. Julie's story, "Infertility: Moving Mountains," 6 June 2013, Stories tab.
C. Eva's Zigzag & 1 podcast interview—Season 2, Episode 22— "In Honor of Holocaust Remembrance Day," 21 Apr. 2020, Podcast tab.
D. Cheryl's Zigzag & 1 podcast interview—Season 3, Episode 45— "Extend Grace," 26 June 2021, Podcast tab.
E. Tami's Zigzag & 1 podcast interview—Season 4, Episode 58— "Even If He Does Not Faith," 11 Apr. 2022, Podcast tab.
F. Cindie's story, "We Trust God," 8 June 2017, Stories tab.
G. Tracy's story, "Nothing Is Impossible," 10 Nov. 2016, Stories tab.
H. Wanda's story, "Bring My Praise," 7 Dec. 2017, Stories tab.
I. Wayne's story, "Double Whammy," 28 June 2015, Stories tab.
J. Rhonda's story, "Collected My Tears," 27 Jan. 2021, Stories tab.
K. Tammy's story, "From Rubble to Royalty," 28 Apr. 2016, Stories tab.
L. Diane's stories, "A No Casserole Illness, Part 1" and "A No Casserole Illness, Part 2," 21 June 2018 and 29 June 2018, respectively, Stories tab.
M. Stephanie's story, "Transformation," 26 April 2019, Stories tab.
N. Chloe's story, "That's Why I Sing," 6 September 2018, Stories tab. Additionally, Chloe gave written permission to use the lyrics of her song "That's Why I Sing."
O. Erin's story, "Broken but Priceless," 27 Sept. 2015, Stories tab.
P. Cori's story, "Source of Hope," 15 Mar. 2018, Stories tab.
Q. Jessica's story, "Look Twice: Save a Life," 2 June 2016, Stories tab.

NOTES

mile 00: Trail Etiquette & Instructions

1. Willard, Nancy. Quoted by Mickey Pearlman and Katherine Usher Henderson, *Inter/View: Talks with America's Writing Women*, The University Press of Kentucky, 2021, 206.
2. Voskamp, Ann. "Unashamed Brokenness." *Faith Gateway Store,* May 13, 2019, www.faithgateway.com/apps/fireamp/blogs/christian-books/unashamed-brokenness. Accessed 15 June 2022.
3. "In Memory of Anthony Bourdain." *YouTube*, uploaded by Tripscout – Travel Entertainment, 4 Jun 2019, www.youtube.com/watch?v=80YWgMzyL4M&t=1s. Accessed 15 June 2022.

mile 01: How Are You Navigating the Unexpected Turns in Your Journey?

1. Walker, Alice. Quoted by Lynne Shayko, "35 Alice Walker Quotes That Will Inspire You to Change the World," *Thought Catalog,* 20 July 2017. www.thoughtcatalog.com/lynne-shayko/2017/07/35-alice-walker-quotes-that-will-inspire-you-to-change-the-world. Accessed 15 June 2022.
2. Naoroji, Caroline. "Testimony." *Smile*Shine*Love,* 17 Dec. 2013, www.smileshinelove.wordpress.com/2013/12/17/testimony. Accessed 15 June 2022.
3. "22 Short Poems About Strength and Courage." *Post Poetics,* www.postpoetics.org/poems-about-strength. Accessed 15 June 2022.
4. Maclaren, Alexander. Quoted in L.B. Cowman, *Streams in the Desert: 366 Devotional Readings,* Zondervan, 1997, 48.

mile 02: Is Struggle Necessary?

1. Keller, Helen. "Optimism 1903." *American Foundation for the Blind*, www.afb.org/about-afb/history/helen-keller/books-essays-speeches/optimism-1903. Accessed 15 June 2022.
2. T.M. Pearce. "The English Proverb in New Mexico." *California Folklore Quarterly* 5 (4), Western States Folklore Society, 1946, 354.

mile 03: Where Are You Setting Up Camp?

1. Hall, Fr Sean. "Seventh Sunday of Easter." *Pauline Books & Media UK*, 15 May 2021, www.paulineuk.org/blog/Liturgical-Reflections/item/Seventh-Sunday-of-Easter. Accessed 15 June 2022.
2. Kipfer, Barbara Ann. *Flip Dictionary: For When You Know What You Want to Say but Can't Think of the Word.* F + W Publications, 2000, 633.
3. "Rack, Shack & Benny." *VeggieTales*, created by Phil Vischer and Mike Nawrocki, Warner Bros. Home Entertainment, 1995.
4. Dalton-Smith, Dr. Saundra. *Sacred Rest: Recover Your Life, Renew Your Energy, Restore Your Sanity.* Faith Works, 2017, 8.
5. Ibid., 15-16.
6. Ortberg, John. *If You Want to Walk on Water You've Got to Get Out of the Boat.* Zondervan, 2001, 150-151.

mile 04: Who Is Guiding Your Journey?

1. Carpenter, Chris. "Christianity as Usual? Not Quite." *CBN*, www1.cbn.com/Christianity-usual-not-quite. Accessed 15 June 2022.
2. DeMille, Nelson. *The Talbot Odyssey.* E-book, Hachette Audio, 2010.
3. Spurgeon, Charles. Quoted by John J, "Four Lessons for Christians Today from the Life and Ministry of Charles Haddon Spurgeon." *Christianity Today*, 01 Feb. 2021, www.christianitytoday.com/article/four.lessons.for.christians.today.from.the.life.and ministry.of.charles.haddon.spurgeon/136308. Accessed 15 June 2022.

mile 05: Who Do You Call on When You're Struggling?

1. Moore, Beth. "It's Prayers. That's the Thing." *Living Proof Ministries*, 4 February 2015, www.blog.lproof.org/2015/02/its-prayer-thats-the-thing. Accessed 15 June 2022.
2. Emerson, Ralph Waldo. Quoted by Lawrence Rosenwald (editor), *Ralph Waldo Emerson: Selected Journals Volume 1 1820-1842*, Library of America, 2010, 203.
3. MacLaine, Erica. "150+ Best Motivational Quotes Images to Achieve Success in Life." *The Best Wishes*, 15 Jan. 2022, www.the-best-wishes.com/motivational-quotes-images. Accessed 15 June 2022.
4. Ruhl, Charlotte. "Bloom's Taxonomy of Learning." *Simply Psychology*, 24 May 2021, www.simplypsychology.org/blooms-taxonomy. Accessed 15 June 2022.
5. Lewis, C.S. Quoted by Pam Farrell, *Woman of Influence: Ten Traits of Those Who Want to Make a Difference*. IVP Books, 2016, 62.

mile 06: Are You Effectively Navigating the Dark?

1. Shakespeare, William. *Henry VI, Part 2*. 1591, 2.1.73-74.
2. "Historical Faith Quotes." *Eyes2C*, www.eyes2c.net/history/historical-faith-quotes. Accessed 15 June 2022.
3. Evans, Dr. Tony. "Treasures in the Darkness." *Proverbs 31 Ministries*, 11 July 2018, www.proverbs31.org/read/devotions/full-post/2018/07/11/treasures-in-the-darkness. Accessed 15 June 2022.

mile 07: Who or What Is Magnified When You See Your Struggles?

1. Gerth, Holley. "When You Need Help Fighting a Battle in Your Life." *Holley Gerth*, www.holleygerth.com/when-you-need-help-fighting-a-battle-in-your-life. Accessed 15 June 2022.
2. Warren, Rick. *The Purpose Driven Life: What on Earth Am I Here For?* Zondervan, 2002, 67.
3. Thrasher, Bill and Lutzer, Erwin W. *A Journey to Victorious Praying: Finding Discipline and Delight in Your Prayer Life*. Moody Publishers, 2017, 214.

mile 08: How Will you Remember Your Journey?

1. Miller, Shelly. *Rhythms of Rest: Finding the Spirit of Sabbath in a Busy World*. Bethany House, 2016, 48.
2. Moore, Beth. *Entrusted: A Study of 2 Timothy*. Life Way Press, 2016, 79.
3. Voskamp, Ann. *One Thousand Gifts: A Dare to Live Fully Right Where You Are*. Zondervan, 2010, 44.
4. Ibid., 225.
5. Merton, Thomas. *New Seeds of Contemplation*. New Directions Books, 1961, 1.
6. Frank, Anne. *The Diary of a Young Girl*. Doubleday, 1976, 197.

Rest & Recharge

1. Cardoza, Benjamin. Quoted by Doug Dickerson, "Rest for the Weary." *Leader's Beacon*, www.leadersbeacon.com/rest-for-the-weary. Accessed 15 June 2022.
2. Cowman, L.B. *Streams in the Desert: 366 Devotional Readings*. Zondervan, 1997, 149.
3. Dalton-Smith, Dr. Saundra. *Sacred Rest: Recover Your Life, Renew Your Energy, Restore Your Sanity*. Faith Works, 2017, 206.

JOURNEY ON QUIZ

How do you navigate the tough challenges that unexpectedly intersect your path?

Your mindset is a powerful indicator of how those challenges will impact your life journey.

Take the quiz at **www.journeyonquiz.com** to discover which journey personality you are!

Want more inspiration to fight to overcome?

Overcomer stories, Zigzag & 1 podcast interviews, and Resources at www.melonybrown.com

FOLLOW Melony

Melony Brown Author

melonybrown_overcomer

**Are you determined to keep moving forward
in your journey of overcoming & thriving?**

KEEP MOVING FORWARD

An Interactive Survival Guide for Overcoming & Thriving
Journey On! SERIES Book 2

Throw your essential gear in your backpack.
Meet Melony at mile marker 09.

The second half of your journey will be far more challenging than the first. You'll need to trust in and rely on your navigator and utilize your gear as you engage with fire, companions, snakes, a first-aid kit, trees, waterfalls, and mirrors.

Let's continue creating your personalized survival guide!

COMING SUMMER 2023

Made in the USA
Columbia, SC
03 November 2022